SCHOLASTIC

Teaching Literary Elements

With Favorite Chapter Books

BY IMMACULA A. RHODES

NEW YORK • TORONTO • LONDON • AUCKLAND • SYDNEY
MEXICO CITY • NEW DELHI • HONG KONG • BUENOS AIRES

Teaching Resources

To Alan and Amber

For adding so much joy

to the story of my life

"Rejoice in the Lord always.

Again I will say, rejoice!"

—PHILIPPIANS 4:4

Cover design by Brian LaRossa
Interior design by Kathy Massaro
Cover and interior artwork by Maxie Chambliss

ISBN-13: 978-0-439-36534-5
ISBN-10: 0-439-36534-1

Copyright © 2007 by Immacula A. Rhodes.
Published by Scholastic Inc.
All rights reserved.
Printed in the U.S.A.

1 2 3 4 5 6 7 8 9 10   40   15 14 13 12 11 10 09 08 07

Contents

Introduction

Welcome to *Teaching Literary Elements With Favorite Chapter Books*—a resource filled with creative activities that encourage students to explore character, plot, setting, and theme in a variety of their favorite books.

This book is designed to help you introduce literary elements to students in a fun, meaningful way. Lessons engage students in discussions and interactive activities that allow them to analyze and interpret information about each particular element. By studying characters, events, places, and themes, students develop an understanding of how stories are structured and how each of these components relates to and affects all the others. Interaction with the text through hands-on activities makes a story come alive for students so that they enjoy richer experiences in reading.

Understanding literary elements helps cultivate students' reading comprehension and story-writing skills. When they examine characters' personalities and behaviors, predict actions and events, analyze settings, and interpret themes, students develop and strengthen their understanding of what they read. The engaging discussions, graphic organizers, and hands-on activities that accompany the lessons in this book allow students to explore each literary element in a variety of ways, challenge them to think beyond the words in the stories, and encourage them to apply what they learn to other works of literature. In addition, when students apply their knowledge of literary elements to their own story creations, they discover that writing can be an enjoyable and rewarding experience. (To see how the lessons and activities in this book link to national and state language arts standards, see page 6.)

A Look Inside

Each section of this book is devoted to one of the four literary elements: character, plot, setting, and theme. The introduction for each section presents an explanation of the literary element, its importance to the story, and a brief example of its use in the featured books. Learning goals are also provided to help you target different facets of the literary element to teach.

In each section, you'll find four children's chapter books that exemplify the targeted literary element. The discussions, activities, and projects in each lesson relate specifically to the featured book, but can be adapted and used with a variety of chapter books. Each lesson includes the following:

Story Summary

This brief description offers an overview of the story and indicates how it connects to the targeted literary element.

Learning Goals

Specific learning objectives for each lesson are listed in this section.

Before Reading

The discussion starters in this section help you introduce and set the stage for reading the book.

After Reading

You can use these discussions, graphic organizers, writing exercises, and other ideas to review the story with students and help them identify aspects of the literary element being studied.

Activities

This section features engaging activities, graphic organizers, and hands-on projects to help students explore the literary element. Each activity includes an introduction, a suggestion for preparing students for the activity, reproducible patterns or activity pages (where applicable), and easy-to-follow directions on how to complete and use the activity or project. You might complete each activity page or project beforehand, and then use it as an example when you present the activity to students.

Projects are designed to give students fun and creative ways to demonstrate and apply what they have learned, while activity pages provide them with interesting ways to express their knowledge through graphic organizers, certificates, letters, and other writing opportunities. All the activities encourage students to reflect on the book, the specific literary element, and their learning experiences.

Integrating This Book Into Your Reading Program

Below are some ways you can incorporate this book into your existing reading program to reinforce and enhance students' experiences with literary elements:

- **Individual Lessons:** Choose the book, learning goals, and/or activities that address what you want to teach. Find the lesson or lessons that best meet your objective. Then select and prepare the lesson components and activities you plan to use. Each lesson is self-contained and includes all the information you need to complete the instruction with students.

- **Lessons With Your Own Books:** Glance through this book to find the lessons that focus on the literary elements you want to teach with your own book. Familiarize yourself with the lessons and plan the parts that need to be adapted for use with your book. You can also use any of the alternate titles listed at the end of the lessons.

Using These Activities With Other Books

To get even more out of the activities, each one can be adapted for use with other chapter books. For example, the personality pizza activity in *Amber Brown Is Not a Crayon* (page 8) can be used to explore the personality traits of characters in many other books. A list of books with which the activity works well is provided for your convenience. You can use books already available in your reading program as well.

Literary Element Mini-Units: Plan a mini-unit to introduce or reinforce students' understanding of a particular literary element. As you plan the unit, decide how many and which books to use (or use your own books), the manner in which students will read the books (individually or as a group), and how much time to allot to the unit and activities.

Extended Literary Elements Unit: You can use all the books and lessons for a particular literary element to teach a longer-term unit on that element. In planning the unit, read the introduction and lessons for the entire unit to establish your goals and decide how much time you want to set aside for the study and the best way to schedule and organize the lessons.

Meeting the Standards for Language Arts

Mid-Continent Research for Education and Learning (McREL), a nationally recognized nonprofit organization, has compiled and evaluated national and state standards—and proposed what teachers should provide for their students to grow proficient in language arts, among other curriculum areas. The lessons and activities in this book support grades 2–4 students in meeting the following McRel standards:

Uses reading skills and strategies to understand and interpret a variety of literary texts

◆ Previews text (skims materials; uses pictures, textual clues, and text format)

◆ Makes, confirms, and revises simple predictions about what will be found in a text

◆ Uses reading skills and strategies to understand and identify the defining characteristics of a variety of literary passages and texts (fiction, fantasies, chapter books)

◆ Understands the basic concept of plot (main problem, conflict, resolution, cause-and-effect)

◆ Understands similarities and differences within and among literary works from various genres (in terms of settings, character types, events, point of view, and the role of natural phenomena)

◆ Understands elements of character development in literary works (differences between main and minor characters; stereotypical characters as opposed to fully developed characters; changes that characters undergo; the importance of a character's actions, motives, and appearance to plot)

◆ Knows themes that recur across literary works

◆ Makes connections between characters or simple events in a literary work and people or events in his or her own life

Uses the general skills and strategies of the writing process including the stylistic and rhetorical aspects of writing

◆ Uses prewriting strategies to plan written work (uses graphic organizers, story maps, and webs; groups related ideas; takes notes; brainstorms ideas; organizes information according to type and purpose of writing)

◆ Writes in response to literature (summarizes main ideas and significant details; relates own ideas to supporting details; advances judgments; supports judgments with references to the text, other works, other authors, nonprint media, and personal knowledge)

◆ Uses descriptive language that clarifies and enhances ideas (common figures of speech, sensory details)

Uses listening and speaking strategies for different purposes

◆ Contributes to group discussions

◆ Responds to questions and comments (gives reasons in support of opinions, responds to others' ideas)

◆ Listens to classmates and adults (asks questions, summarizes or paraphrases to confirm understanding, gives feedback)

Kendall, J. S., & Marzano, R. J. (2004). *Content knowledge: A compendium of standards and benchmarks for K–12 education.* Aurora, CO: Mid-continent Research for Education and Learning. Online database: http://www.mcrel.org/standards-benchmarks/.

CHARACTER

Character is the magnet that attracts readers to a story—and the force that pulls them deeper into the story. Often the main character reminds readers of themselves or of people they know. This familiarity allows them to make a personal connection to the character and helps them identify with his or her hopes, needs, values, questions, weaknesses, problems, feelings, and actions. By getting to know and understand the character, students are able to relate their own personalities, traits, and experiences to those of the character—they get a glimpse of themselves in the form of the character. With character being the most important channel through which readers interact with a story, this unit makes a natural place for students to begin their studies of literary elements.

The books in this section introduce students to a variety of characters: Amber Brown, the strong-willed but sensitive third-grader; Peter Hatcher, whose patience is constantly being tested by his younger brother; the lonely "new kid" Leigh Botts; and Stanley Yelnats, the unlucky good guy. You can use the discussion and activities related to their stories to help students accomplish the following learning goals:

* Examine the character's actions, feelings, thoughts, likes, and dislikes to learn about and understand the character's personality

* Express understanding of a character through language-building activities such as character cases, journal writing, and dramatizations

* Develop a deeper understanding of a character through activities such as creating a personality pizza, making an emotions makeover machine, and completing character recognition certificates

* Infer traits, thoughts, feelings, values, and motivations of a character through activities such as making slide-through character quotes, creating comic strips, and constructing a "hidden" traits game

Introducing Character

To launch a study on character, you might do one or more of the following with students:

* Write and circle the name of one of their favorite book characters in the middle of a sheet of chart paper. Invite volunteers to create a character web by adding words that describe the character and drawing lines from the words to the name.

* Describe the physical and personality traits of a book character familiar to students. Ask them to identify the character and then name other features or traits that represent the character.

* Have students name a favorite book character and tell what qualities make that character memorable. Create a chart to sort the qualities by physical traits, personality traits, feelings, and actions. Use the chart to help students understand that many different characteristics can represent a character.

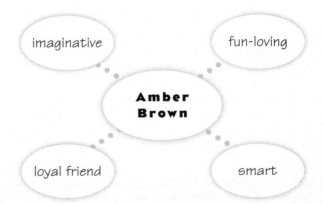

Amber Brown
Is Not a Crayon

by Paula Danziger

❖❖

(G. P. PUTNAM'S SONS, 1994)

Learning Goals

❀ Describe a character by examining her words, thoughts, and actions.

❀ Create a personality pizza to explore the traits that make a character unique.

❀ Show understanding of a character's feelings with slide-through character quotes.

Ever since kindergarten, Amber Brown and Justin Daniels have been a great team. These two best friends are practically inseparable as they help and watch out for each other, share cookies and games, and read each other's mind. But during their third-grade school year, Justin learns he must move away. That's when the fighting begins and the two stop talking to each other. Will these ex-best friends be able to work out their differences and renew the friendship before Justin goes away for good? Students will easily identify with the strong-willed, straightforward Amber Brown as they focus on how this character reveals herself in everyday situations.

Before Reading

Have any students had to say good-bye to a close friend who moved far away? Invite them to share their experiences and emotions related to the event. Were they sad? Angry? Confused? Did they try to pretend the separation wasn't really going to happen? Or did they act out by picking a fight with their friend?

Ask students who have not had this experience to add their thoughts to the discussion. Afterward, show students the cover of *Amber Brown Is Not a Crayon*. Explain that this story describes how one third-grader handles the reality of her best friend moving away.

After Reading

Ask students what they think of Amber Brown. Is she a character they would like to know? Would she make a good best friend? Why or why not? After students share their thoughts, help them focus on the traits that make Amber Brown a unique individual.

1. On a sheet of chart paper, draw a circle with spokes extending from it. Write "Amber Brown" in the circle.

2. Ask students to brainstorm words or phrases that describe Amber Brown, reminding them that a character's traits might be positive and appealing or they might be unattractive qualities. Write their responses on the spokes, adding more spokes as needed.

3. When finished, invite students to group into pairs and use words from the character word web to describe Amber Brown to their partners.

My Character's Personality Pizza

Amber Brown is a unique and colorful character with whom students can easily identify. Use this activity to help students examine Amber's personality traits and discover how these are expressed in her actions and words.

For each student:

✿ copy of page 10
✿ crayons or colored pencils
✿ scissors
✿ large paper plate

Introducing the Activity

1. Amber Brown loves pizza. In fact, she knows very well what she thinks, feels, likes, and dislikes about most everything. Help students make a list of her character traits. Then invite them to share examples of how Amber demonstrates each trait. For instance, her refusal to talk to Justin is an example of being stubborn. The clutter in her desk supports her self-admission to being messy. Explain that each trait, if taken in isolation, can apply to many different people. But when they are all brought together and combined, they create a very unique individual—Amber Brown.

2. To demonstrate how many different traits create a whole personality, invite students to create a pizza with slices that represent different pieces of Amber Brown's personality. Later, to extend the activity, students can create pizzas that represent themselves.

Making the Pizza

1. Give students a copy of page 10. Ask them to choose five character traits that describe Amber Brown and have them write each trait on a separate mushroom on their pizza. Then have students write on each sausage circle a phrase that tells what Amber says, does, or thinks that supports the trait labeled on the mushroom.

2. Have students color their pizzas and cut the slices apart.

3. Instruct students to write "Amber Brown" in the middle of a paper plate. Then, working with a partner, have them put a pizza together on the plate, one slice at a time. As they place each slice, ask students to share additional actions, words, or thoughts that indicate that Amber Brown possesses the trait named on the mushroom. Also encourage them to discuss how Amber's personality might be different if a particular slice was missing from the whole pizza, or if she did not possess the specific trait represented on each slice.

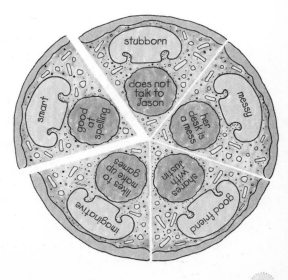

My Character's Personality Pizza

Slide-Through Character Quotes

Amber Brown experiences many different emotions in the story. She names some of her feelings very specifically in her narrative, but leaves the reader to infer others. This activity helps students identify and express Amber's emotions in quotes written from the character's perspective.

Introducing the Activity

Ask students if they are familiar with the phrase "emotional roller coaster." Invite them to share their understanding of the phrase. Then discuss how Amber Brown's experiences caused her emotions to rise and fall, much like a roller-coaster ride. Have students name some of Amber's emotional highs and lows in the story. How might Amber describe each of her emotional experiences in a sentence? To share their responses, invite students to make these slide-through character quotes.

Making the Slide-Through Character Quotes

1. Give students copies of page 12. Ask them to cut out the quote strip and character page and cut the two slits on the character page where indicated. Then have them draw a picture of Amber Brown under the speech bubble and write her name on the line.

2. Encourage students to imagine what Amber Brown might say she feels about a specific event in the story. For example, she might say, "I got so mad at Justin because he wouldn't talk about his move." Or "When Justin and I became friends again, I felt so relieved!" Have them write a quote, in Amber's words, in each section of their quote strip.

3. To complete the project, direct students to thread their quote strips between the two slits, as shown. To use it, they slide the strip up or down so that one quote at a time appears on the speech bubble. Encourage students to share their slide-through quotes with classmates.

For each student:

- copy of page 12
- scissors
- crayons or colored pencils

Other Books to Use With These Activities

The Adventures of Ali Baba Bernstein
by Johanna Hurwitz
(William Morrow and Company, 1985)

Judy Moody
by Megan McDonald
(Candlewick Press, 2000)

Pippi Longstocking
by Astrid Lindgren
(Viking Press, 1950)

Slide-Through Character Quotes

How did .... feel?

(character name)

Teaching Literary Elements With Favorite Chapter Books © 2007 by Immacula A. Rhodes, Scholastic Teaching Resources

Tales of a Fourth Grade Nothing

by Judy Blume

(PENGUIN BOOKS FOR YOUNG READERS, 1972)

Peter's biggest problem isn't his mother, his father, or even school. His biggest problem is his two-year-old brother, Fudge. Although his parents and everyone else think Fudge is adorable, Peter is running low on patience and tolerance for his bratty brother's temper tantrums, silly games, and meddling ways. Then one day Fudge goes too far and his mischief puts him and Peter's pet turtle in danger. This story introduces students to a character who tries to rely on his positive traits to deal with the challenges of a younger sibling's behavior.

Learning Goals

❀ Identify key traits of a character's personality.

❀ Explore how a character responds to different situations.

❀ Extend understanding of a character's feelings about his or her situation.

Before Reading

Poll students to find out how many have younger brothers or sisters. Ask these students to raise their hands if they have ever had an argument, disagreement, or problem with the younger children in their homes. (Most likely all of them will put up their hands!) Then invite them to share their sibling-conflict experiences with the class.

☀ How did they feel about the situation? How did they solve the conflict? Did the solution work well for everyone involved?

Afterward, tell students that they will read a story to learn how a big brother handles conflicts with his mischievous two-year-old brother.

After Reading

Ask the class what they think about Peter and the way he dealt with Fudge's antics and accidents.

☀ Did he respond in an acceptable way?

☀ How might he have responded differently?

☀ What would they do in each situation?

Invite student pairs to act out scenarios between Peter and Fudge in which Peter responds in a different way than he does in the story. To extend the activity, have students create Peter and Fudge stick puppets to act out actual events from the story, revised versions, or their own made-up events.

Materials

For each student:

❀ copy of page 15

❀ crayons or colored pencils

Turtle Traits

In *Tales of a Fourth Grade Nothing*, Peter finds himself in one conflict after another; each initiated by or related to the behavior of his younger brother, Fudge. These challenging situations require Peter to rely on some character traits more than others in order to resolve the conflicts successfully. Use the turtle traits activity to help students determine up to four major character traits that influence Peter's responses and reactions to the different situations he faces.

Introducing the Activity

1. Explain that many words can be used to describe Peter's character, but some traits stand out more than others, especially when he or his parents faced difficult, challenging, or uncomfortable situations with Fudge. For example, Peter can be considered both a teaser and a polite person. However, the polite trait of his character takes over when his mother asks him to stop calling his brother "Fang" (although he continues to think the name in his mind!). Peter is also stubborn, but helpful. So when his dad asks him to ride the Toddle-Bike, he reluctantly complies to help his dad out of an awkward situation.

2. Encourage students to think of other situations in which Peter exhibits strong positive traits, such as responsibility, a sense of humor, and patience. Have them use what they learn about Peter to complete the turtle traits activity.

Using the Turtle Traits Activity Page

1. Give students copies of page 15. Instruct them to write "Peter Hatcher" on the turtle's head.

2. Ask students to think of words that describe the strongest traits of Peter's character—traits that helped him cope with, overcome, or avoid conflicts with Fudge. Have them choose the four most outstanding traits and then write each of these on a different turtle leg.

3. Encourage students to recall examples of how Peter demonstrated the character trait identified on each turtle leg. Have them write one or more examples on the section of the turtle shell next to the corresponding leg.

4. Invite students to color and then share their turtles with the class.

Turtle Traits

Peter Hatcher
character

helpful
trait

sense of humor
trait

responsible
trait

polite
trait

He helped his mother with Fudge's birthday party. He helped with shoe shopping and at the dentist, too.

Peter and his mother laughed about the birthday party. He laughed with his dad about the weekend his mom went away.

Peter took care of his turtle, Dribble. He did his homework. Then he did it again when Fudge ruined it.

He thanked Mrs. Yarby for a present he didn't like. Peter said his dad's omelet was okay when it really tasted bad.

Turtle Traits

character

trait

trait

trait

trait

For each student:

- 8 ½ - by 11-inch sheet of white copy paper
- scissors
- colored pencils or markers

Character Comic Strip

To readers, Fudge's antics may seem comical, but Peter had strong feelings and opinions about how his brother's behavior impacted him personally. In this activity, students will explore Peter's feelings about and reactions to different situations in the story.

Introducing the Activity

1. Create a three-column chart (see sample, below) on which to record different situations from the story, Peter's reactions to and feelings about those situations, and the outcomes. Have students help fill in the chart and then discuss Peter's response to each situation listed. How strong was his reaction? Did his response impact the outcome?

2. Next, show students several samples of comic strips (Peanuts comic strips are a good choice for this activity). Point out how the "story" and the characters' feelings are often communicated through dialogue bubbles that enclose the characters' words or thoughts. Tell students that some comic strips use captions above or below each frame to describe or explain the illustrations. Also identify ways in which comic strips might emphasize any strong feelings experienced by a character. For instance, the illustrations might include facial and body expressions to communicate anger, fear, or frustration. The character's words might also be capitalized or printed in bold letters.

3. Afterward, tell students that they will create their own story-related comic strips using information from the chart.

Situation	Peter's Reaction or Feeling	Outcome
Fudge got into Peter's room and ruined his poster.	Peter got mad and yelled at his mother. He said he hated Fudge.	Fudge got spanked. Peter had to start over on his poster.
Fudge got picked for the Toddle-Bike commercial, but he wouldn't ride the bike.	Peter was jealous that Fudge got picked. But then he helped by showing Fudge how to ride.	Fudge rode the bike finally. Peter got a kiss—yuck!
Fudge swallowed Peter's turtle, Dribble.	Peter blamed his mother. He was upset that no one cared about what happened to Dribble.	Fudge went to the hospital until they got the turtle out of him. Peter got a puppy!

Making the Comic Strip

1. Have students cut a sheet of 8 ½- by 11-inch white paper in half lengthwise. Instruct them to glue the two strips together at one end to make a single, long strip of paper. Then have them divide the strip into a six-part comic-strip frame. (To do this, they can fold the strip into thirds, then in half, and then unfold it. They can then draw lines to delineate the sections.)

2. Ask students to pick a situation from the chart that elicited a strong reaction or feeling from Peter, such as when Fudge ruined his project poster. Tell them to think about how they might illustrate the situation, Peter's response, and the outcome in the six frames on their paper strips.

3. Then help students decide whether they want to "tell" the story using the characters' words in thought and speech bubbles, in captions, or with a combination of the two. After students mentally organize their comic strips, invite them to illustrate their selected situations in their six-part frames. As they work, remind students that they might also use illustrations and capital or bold lettering to help emphasize Peter's response to the situation.

4. After students have completed their comic strips, encourage them to share their comics with classmates and then display them in the classroom.

Dear Mr. Henshaw

by Beverly Cleary

❖

(WILLIAM MORROW AND COMPANY, 1983)

Learning Goals

❀ Explore a character's feelings and how they change.

❀ Discover different traits about a character by looking at how that person presents himself or herself.

❀ Create and pack a character case with interesting information about a character.

To fulfill a class assignment, Leigh Botts writes a letter to his longtime favorite author, Boyd Henshaw. When the author replies, Leigh continues the correspondence, first with actual letters and later in a diary. Through sharing with the real and "pretend" Mr. Henshaw, the lonely boy discovers an outlet for expressing his feelings about being the new kid at school, missing his truck-driver dad, and having a thief take the good things from his lunch every day. Little did Leigh know that his letter-writing habit would also help him resolve his problems and find his own place in the world. In his own words, Leigh introduces readers to his life story and his personal thoughts and feelings.

Before Reading

Why does a "new kid" often have difficulty making friends and fitting in to a new school? Invite students to share their responses to this question. Then explain that fitting in to a new setting is never easy, and can be made even more difficult when differences such as backgrounds, experiences, interests, abilities, learning styles, and even looks and personality are involved. Ask:

✸ Have any of you experienced any of these difficulties firsthand? How did you adjust?

✸ Did a special person, thing, action, or attitude help you find how and where you fit in to the new situation?

After sharing, tell students that they will read a book consisting of a series of letters that describe a young boy's experience in adjusting to a new home, life, and school.

1. Invite students to talk about the ways in which Leigh's writing helped him express and work out his feelings and problems. Then ask if any of them keep a journal. If so, have those students tell about the advantages of writing their thoughts and feelings in a journal.

2. Have students create journals by stapling a stack of white paper between two construction paper covers. Let them decorate and personalize the covers. Then challenge students to record daily their experiences, feelings, and thoughts related to any difficult situations, conflicts, or worries in their lives.

3. After several weeks, invite students to tell whether or not their journal-writing experiences helped them to see their situations or themselves differently. Did they solve any problems or make significant changes in their feelings or behavior as a result? Did they make new discoveries about themselves? Encourage students to continue writing in their journals throughout the year.

Emotions Makeover Machine

Leigh is a character who was struggling with several different situations and emotions at the same time. This activity encourages students to think about Leigh's feelings and the events that helped change them.

Introducing the Activity

For each student:

✿ copy of page 21

✿ scissors

✿ crayons, colored pencils, or markers

✿ glue

1. Ask students if they have ever seen before-and-after pictures of people who have made improvements to themselves, such as a new haircut, a different wardrobe, or weight loss. Explain that these kinds of improvements are often called makeovers. Then tell students that people can also have emotional makeovers, in which something happens—perhaps a change in their actions or attitudes—to help improve their feelings about certain things. Compare some of Leigh's feelings about his situation at the beginning of the book to his feelings at the end. Did he experience an emotional makeover?

2. Invite students to make emotions makeover machines to explore Leigh's feelings and the events that helped changed them. Later, students might also make emotion makeover machines to explore their own before-and-after feelings about different situations, or those of a character from another book.

Making the Emotions Makeover Machine

1. Give students copies of page 21. Have them cut out the emotions makeover machine and the before-and-after writing strips. Instruct them to color the machine, cut along the slits at both ends, and then glue the two writing strips together where indicated. Direct students to thread the single long strip through the slits in the machine, as shown.

2. To fill out the writing strip, students should slide the "before" section to the left of the machine. Beside each number, have them write about a feeling that Leigh experienced during the early parts of the story and what caused him to feel that way. For instance, "Leigh was lonely because he didn't have any friends." Have students draw a simple picture to illustrate that feeling in the corresponding box.

3. Next to each corresponding number on the machine itself, have students write about an event or action that helped Leigh change the feeling named on the "before" section (this represents his emotional makeover). For the above example, they might write "Leigh helped a kid in his class make an alarm, and they became friends."

4. Ask students to slide the writing strip to the right so that the "after" section shows. Next, have them write about Leigh's feelings after he experienced his makeover. For instance, "He was glad to have a new friend." Finally, students should draw a picture in each box to represent Leigh's new, improved feeling.

5. Invite students to use their emotions makeover machine to retell parts of the story.

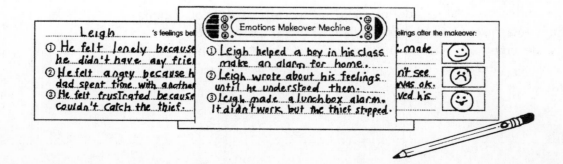

.... 's feelings before the makeover:

① ....

② ....

③ ....

.... 's feelings after the makeover:

① ....

② ....

③ ....

Emotions Makeover Machine

① ....

② ....

③ ....

Teaching Literary Elements With Favorite Chapter Books © 2007 by Immacula A. Rhodes, Scholastic Teaching Resources

Other Books to Use With These Activities

Because of Winn-Dixie
by Kate DiCamillo
(Candlewick Press, 2000)

The Chalk Box Kid
by Clyde Robert Bulla
(Random House, 1987)

There's a Boy in the Girl's Bathroom
by Louis Sachar
(Alfred A. Knopf, 1987)

Character Case

Leigh revealed a lot about himself by answering a list of questions sent by Mr. Henshaw. The activity below invites students to reveal what they know about a favorite book character by creating a case full of information about that character.

Introducing the Activity

Tell students that they are going to create a character case for Leigh Botts or another book character of their choice. Explain that they will pretend to be the character and answer the same questions that Mr. Henshaw asked Leigh. (No peeking at the answers in the book for students who decide to use Leigh as their character!) Students will pack the answers in a special case until they are ready to share the information about their character with the class. To extend the activity, you might also ask students to create character cases for made-up characters or even for themselves.

Making the Character Case

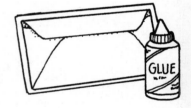

1. Instruct students to color and cut out the character case and pencils on page 23. Have them glue the front of a letter-size envelope to the back of the case (the envelope flap should be loose so that it can be lifted to insert the pencil cutouts).

2. Have students write the name of a book character on the character case. Then ask them to read the question on each pencil and answer it—from their character's perspective—on a blank card, using both the front and back as needed. (There may not be an answer to every question for their selected character. In those instances, you might want to substitute a different question for any that can't be answered.)

3. Afterward, instruct students to staple each pencil to its answer card. Have them pack their cards in the character case by inserting them into the attached envelope.

4. Students may use their character cases in a variety of ways:

❋ They might use the questions and answers to introduce their character as part of a book report.

❋ They can write a new version of the story using information from the character case.

❋ By keeping the identity of the book characters a secret, students can play a game of Guess Who, sharing the answers to the questions with classmates (of course, they will need to omit the pencil labeled "Who are you?").

❋ Students might include illustrations of their characters along with the character cases to create an interactive display in which viewers can remove and read information from the character cases.

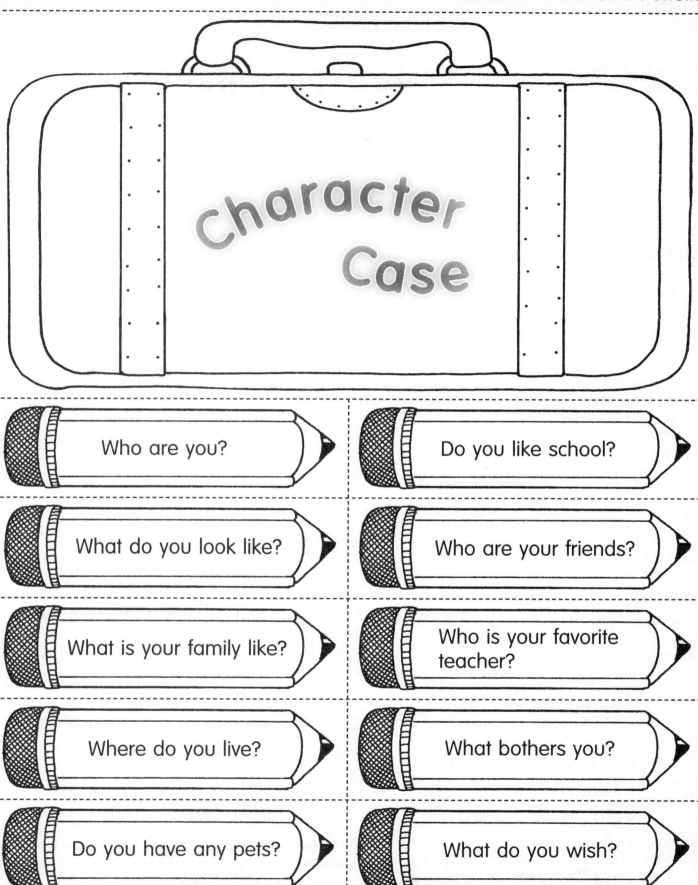

Character Case

Who are you?

Do you like school?

What do you look like?

Who are your friends?

What is your family like?

Who is your favorite teacher?

Where do you live?

What bothers you?

Do you have any pets?

What do you wish?

Holes

by Louis Sachar

❖

(RANDOM HOUSE, 1998)

Thanks to his pig-stealing great-great-grandfather, Stanley Yelnats is under the curse that has followed his family for generations. So when he is sentenced to serve time at Camp Green Lake, Stanley isn't surprised to discover there is no lake there. Instead, the hard, flat wasteland of the camp is filled with holes, which were dug by the boys under the camp warden's command. But after days of digging, Stanley realizes there's more to the warden's purpose than meets the eye—she's looking for something! As Stanley tries to dig up the truth, he unknowingly triggers events that will change his destiny forever! Readers are introduced to a quiet character whose many hidden—and surprising—traits are revealed as the story unfolds.

Learning Goals

✿ Explore how and why a character changes in a story.

✿ Discover hidden personality traits by examining a character's thoughts, words, and actions.

✿ Extend understanding of a character by examining how he or she faces a problem in the story.

Home	Camp Green Lake
imagination	imagination
lonely— no friends	had "friends"— one good friend
unlucky	unlucky
hopeful	hopeful
afraid of bullies— avoided them	nervous about bullies but didn't avoid them
honest	didn't always tell truth
told on bullies	kept quiet—didn't tell
sense of humor about being unlucky	sense of humor left him for a while
caring	became hard-hearted
cooperative— not a bad kid	cooperative—not a troublemaker
target of teasing by Derrick	target of teasing by other boys

Before Reading

Ask students if they have ever been blamed for doing something that they didn't do. If so, how did they handle the accusation? Were they able to convince others that they were innocent? Or did they have to suffer correction or punishment as if they were guilty? Invite students to share their experiences and to describe how they felt about the situation. Afterward, tell them that they will meet a boy in *Holes* who had to "do the time" for a crime he didn't commit.

After Reading

Make a two-column chart and label the columns "Home" and "Camp Green Lake." Explain that, in the story, some parts of Stanley's personality remained the same after he left home for camp, but other parts changed. For instance, in both settings he tried to do his best and was cooperative. However, when he was home, he complained about and avoided bullies, but at camp he kept quiet and tolerated them.

As a class, review and list the things students know about Stanley from both his home life and life at camp. Then ask students to compare the items in each column.

* Are there facets of Stanley's personality that changed between the two settings? What are they? How and why did they change? Were the changes positive or negative?

* Do students think Stanley might change these parts of his personality again in the future? (For example, will he be dishonest to avoid being rejected or bullied by others in the future?) Ask them to explain their answers.

* Finally, have students evaluate the overall changes in Stanley's personality and tell whether or not they make him a better person.

The "Hole" Personality Game

Stanley Yelnats is a complicated character with many unnamed and unseen personality traits. With this activity, students will examine Stanley's character more closely to discover hidden traits and to develop a better understanding of his personality.

Introducing the Activity

1. In reading *Holes*, students learn about some of Stanley's personality traits because they are named or easily detected throughout the story. For example, the author explains that Stanley is hopeful. Readers also learn that he's honest, since he follows his mother's advice to tell the truth. Ask students to list these and other noticeable traits of Stanley's personality on a chart. After generating this list, read it aloud.

2. Next, encourage students to dig deeper into Stanley's personality by reviewing some of his greatest challenges. What did his response to these situations reveal about him? For example, what character trait did Stanley demonstrate when he discovered the warden's motive behind making the boys dig holes? (*intelligence*) When he set out across the dry land alone? (*courage*) When he joked about the restaurant on Big Thumb? (*sense of humor*) When he carried Zero up the mountain? (*loyalty*)

3. As students discover Stanley's "hidden" personality traits, add them to the list. Afterward, invite students to make and play the following game to develop a better understanding of Stanley's whole personality.

For each student:

* 9- by 12-inch sheet of black construction paper
* 12- by 18-inch sheet of white construction paper
* paper or plastic drinking cup
* scissors
* tape
* glue and sand (optional)

For each student pair:

* penny
* supply of small sticky notes

Making the Game

1. Give each of the students a 9- by 12-inch sheet of black construction paper and a plastic cup. Instruct them to trace the mouth of the cup 12 times on the black paper and then cut out the circles.

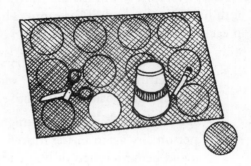

2. Have students use a short piece of tape to attach the circles to a 12- by 18-inch sheet of white construction paper (as shown), creating round black flaps (these represent black holes in a dry desert). Then students should trace around each hole with a pencil so that the outline of a circle appears when the flap is lifted.

3. Ask students to write one of Stanley's "hidden" personality traits under any six holes. Remind them that these are traits that are not explicitly stated in the story. Also have them write about how Stanley demonstrated that trait—through his thoughts, words, or actions. When finished, six holes will have writing under them and six will not. If desired, students can glue sand on the white paper around the holes to represent the dry, hard land.

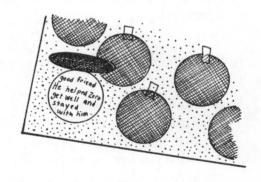

4. To play, pair up students and give each pair a penny and a supply of small sticky notes.

   ❋ Partners take turns tossing the penny onto each other's game board.

   ❋ When the penny lands on a hole, the player lifts the flap. If one of Stanley's personality traits is hidden under it, the player reads the information, closes the flap, and tags the hole with a sticky note.

   ❋ If the hole is empty, the flap is closed and the turn ends.

   ❋ The first player to tag all six holes hiding Stanley's personality traits is the winner!

Thumbs-Up! Certificate

In the story, Stanley had to face—and try to overcome—a number of problems created by his situation, the environment, or other characters. This activity allows students to recognize Stanley for his accomplishments and positive character traits. Students might also use the certificate to recognize the achievements and positive qualities of other story characters or of classmates.

Materials

For each student:

✿ copy of page 28

✿ scissors

Introducing the Activity

1. Ask students to explain what they think a certificate of recognition is. Then, explain that this is often given to someone who makes a significant accomplishment. The certificate represents a sort of thumbs-up approval of what the person achieved.

2. Ask students to think about Stanley's predicament. Did he face problems? What caused his problems? Did he overcome his problems to accomplish anything significant? What character traits did he rely on to succeed? Ask students to explain their responses. After discussing, invite students to prepare certificates of achievement to give Stanley a thumbs-up for his successes.

Using the Thumbs Up! Certificate

1. Provide students with a copy of the certificate on page 28. If desired, have them cut out the hand on the page.

2. Ask students to think about a problem that Stanley faced and eventually solved—something for which they'd like to give him thumbs-up approval. Encourage them to decide what personality trait most helped him overcome that problem. Then have students complete the "To" and "For" lines of the certificate. On the remaining lines, ask them to explain—to Stanley—why he is being recognized for that particular accomplishment and the personality trait that contributed to his success.

3. Invite students to complete several certificates to recognize Stanley for different accomplishments. Or have them fill out certificates to recognize positive traits in other characters of their choice.

Other Books to Use With These Activities

Frindle
by Andrew Clements
(Simon & Schuster, 1996)

Just Juice
by Karen Hesse
(Scholastic Press, 1998)

Maniac Magee
by Jerry Spinelli
(HarperTrophy, 1990)

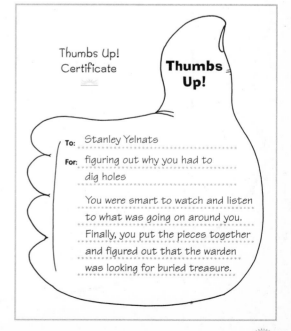

Thumbs Up! Certificate

Thumbs Up!

To: Stanley Yelnats

For: figuring out why you had to dig holes

You were smart to watch and listen to what was going on around you. Finally, you put the pieces together and figured out that the warden was looking for buried treasure.

Thumbs-Up! Certificate

Thumbs Up!

To: ....

For: ....

....

....

....

....

....

PLOT

The plot of a story consists of an initial conflict, a series of related events, and a logical conclusion to the problem. In short, the plot includes what happens in a story and why. It is the literary element that hooks readers and keeps them interested. A well-developed plot establishes and builds complications around a major conflict. As the plot progresses toward its resolution, it involves turning points—or critical events—that may result in setbacks, challenges, disappointments, discoveries, or successes for the main character or characters. Plot is the literary element most useful in building and strengthening students' comprehension skills. An engaging plot encourages students to discuss, analyze, evaluate, and express their feelings or opinions about events and character actions. The ongoing action challenges them to make cause-and-effect connections and predictions about future events. The resolution prompts students to summarize and determine whether the story's results are reasonable and satisfactory.

In this section, students are introduced to a variety of plots driven by different forces. In *How to Eat Fried Worms*, the plot grows out of the characters' motives and related actions. *Bunnicula* features a plot steered by a character's imagination, while in *Bud, Not Buddy*, the plot develops from events related to a character's circumstances. In *Mr. Popper's Penguins*, a humorous chain of cause-and-effect events drives the plot. As students explore plot with the books and activities in this section, it might be helpful to review with them the steps that make up a traditional story structure:

※ The opening of a story typically introduces the characters and presents the initial conflict. The reader usually learns what problem the main character faces in the first few chapters of the book.

※ Subsequent chapters consist of complications that arise as the main character tries to resolve the conflict. These complications might create new problems for the character to solve or magnify the initial problem.

※ The climax, usually the most exciting event in story, is reached when a character has to choose a way to settle the initial conflict. This may involve a decision, action, or understanding that grows out of the story complications and results in solving the conflict.

※ A resolution is reached, and the problem is solved. The story ends by summing up how the characters feel and what they do now that the conflict is resolved.

This section provides activities—such as discussion starters, diagrams, charts, and dramatizations—to help students explore a variety of plots. Additional activities involving storytelling, book-making, letter-writing, and board games help reinforce students' understanding of plot, as well as invite them to extend familiar stories in fun, creative ways.

How to Eat Fried Worms

by Thomas Rockwell

❖

(FRANKLIN WATTS, 1973)

Learning Goals

❀ Understand how a plot is driven by the minds and motives of characters.

❀ Explore the plot to identify the discoveries, setbacks, and successes of the characters.

❀ Recognize a plot as a series of events, beginning with an initial problem and ending with a resolution.

When Billy makes a bet to eat a worm a day for 15 days, his opponents eagerly supply him with the earth-dwelling entrées. Determined to win, he downs the first worms with much discomfort and great concern for his health. But with moral support from friends and family, and a number of creative ways to prepare the wormy meals, Billy finds the crawlers easier to swallow with each passing day. As his once-confident opponents watch him close in on the $50 winnings, they desperately devise one plan after another to ensure his failure. This delightfully disgusting tale introduces readers to a plot based on character motives and the conflicts that arise from them.

Before Reading

Tell students that they are going to read a story about a boy who made a bet to eat 15 worms. Ask them if they would ever make a similar bet.

☀ If yes, why would they bet something like that? Under what conditions would they make the bet?

☀ Would the worms be alive or dead? Would they eat the worms raw?

☀ What would be the payoff for winning the bet? To prove a point? A special privilege? Money?

After discussing, read the first chapter of the book aloud to discover Billy's motive for accepting the challenge.

After Reading

Invite students to share their reactions to the story. Then have them look more closely at the sequence of events.

☀ Explain that the story begins with an initial conflict. Draw the outline of a large mountain on the chalkboard, and write the initial problem on the left side of the base.

☀ Next, tell students that the events that build interest and excitement, and ultimately lead to the solution to the problem, are called the rising action. Ask volunteers to name some of these events and write them along the left slope of the mountain.

✹ Ask students to describe the turning point of the story, or climax. Write this on the mountain peak.

✹ Along the right slope of the mountain, write students' responses to what happened after the climax to solve the problem—the falling action.

✹ Finally, on the right side of the mountain base, write the resolution, or the part of the story in which the characters adjust to the solution. Use the diagram to explain how story plots are typically developed.

Twists-and-Turns Plot Booklet

The four boys start out as friends at the beginning of the story, but their determination to win the bet turns them into enemies as they spring unexpected surprises on each other. This activity helps students identify how a story's plot can take unexpected twists and turns before reaching a resolution.

Introducing the Activity

Ask students if the boys in the story carried out the bet without any complications. If not, what kinds of things caused complications? Were the boys surprised by some of the complications? Why? How did these events make the story more interesting and exciting? Explain to students that complications in a plot can create twists and turns that make it more exciting and interesting. Then invite them to make these plot booklets to identify complications in the story.

Making the Booklet

1. Ask students to cut out the booklet pages on page 32, plus several additional copies of the "Complication" sections.

2. Instruct students to write the story's initial conflict on the page with the worm's head and the resolution on the page with the worm's tail. They should use separate sections of the worm's body to write down a complication related to the story's initial conflict along with the solution to each complication. They may include several pages, but encourage students to make a page only for each major complication, not for minor ones.

3. Have students sequence their booklet pages. Ask them to glue or tape the pages together end to end, with the head of the worm at the left end and the tail at the right. The resulting strip will resemble a wiggly worm that represents the twists and turns in the story's plot.

4. Direct students to accordion-fold their booklets so that the worm's head is on top. Invite them to use their booklets to retell the story.

Materials

For each student:

❁ copy of page 32 (with extra copies of the "Complication" sections)

❁ scissors

❁ glue stick or tape

Twists-and-Turns Plot Booklet

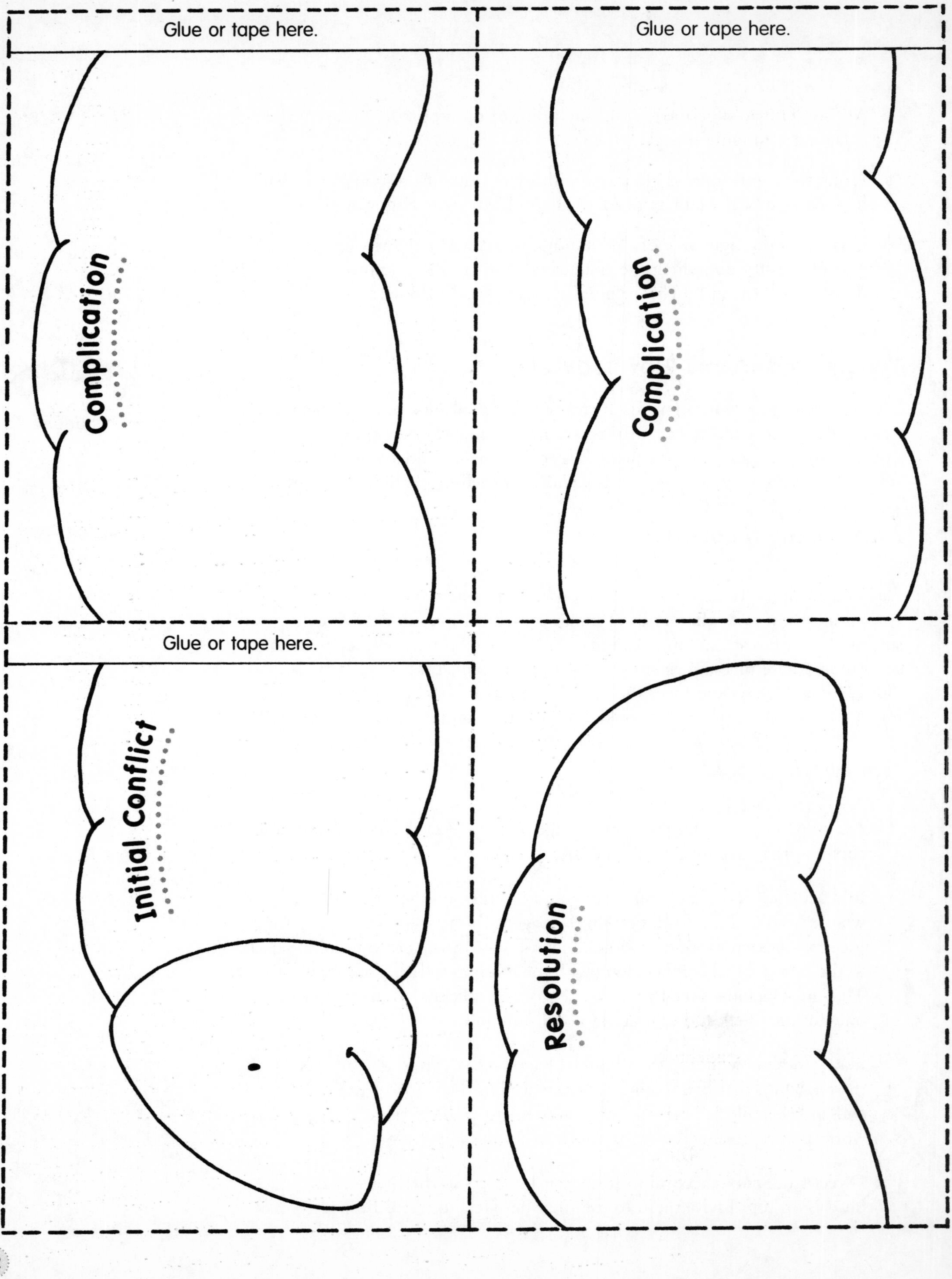

Glue or tape here.
Complication
Glue or tape here.
Complication
Glue or tape here.
Initial Conflict
Resolution

Persuasion Letter

The plot of *How to Eat Fried Worms* is directed and driven by the characters' motives, decisions, and actions. In this activity, students will write letters to persuade a character to change his or her mind or behavior, and then explore possible plot shifts that might occur as a result of the change.

Introducing the Activity

1. Ask students to tell how the plot might shift, or change completely, given different events. For example:

   * if someone convinced Billy not to eat any more worms
   * if Alan was persuaded to stop trying to make Billy lose the bet
   * if Tom or Joe were talked out of taking any part in the bet
   * if Billy's mom was encouraged to make him stop eating the worms

2. After discussing ways in which these scenarios might influence the plot, have students write a persuasion letter to convince one of the characters that he or she should change a particular behavior and to explain how that might affect the story.

Writing the Letter

1. Encourage students to select a character whose behavior they feel needs to be changed, and then address the letter on page 34 to that character.

2. Have students begin the letter by telling the character about the targeted behavior. Instruct them to complete the sentence in the top section by writing what they believe the character currently thinks, feels, wants, plans, or hopes for.

3. Ask students to think about how they would advise the character to change his or her behavior. Instruct them to complete the sentence in the middle section by writing ways in which the character should change.

4. Next, have students complete the sentence in the bottom section by writing how the new behavior might change a specific part of the story or the entire story.

5. Finally, have students sign their letters. Later, invite them to share their letters with the class.

Materials

For each student:

❀ copy of page 34

Other Books
to Use With
These Activities

Chocolate-Covered Ants
by Stephen Manes
(Scholastic, 1990)

The Chocolate Touch
by Patrick Skene Catling
(Morrow Junior Books, 1979)

Freckle Juice
by Judy Blume
(Four Winds Press, 1971)

Persuasion Letter

May 15, 2007
(date)

Dear Alan ,
(character)

I know you don't want to lose the bet and have to give Billy the money. That would make your dad mad and make you poor.

Before anything else happens, I want to encourage you to be fair and stop making up lies to scare Billy or trick him. You need to be honest and let Billy try his best.

If you do this, then Billy will probably let you keep some of the money if he wins, or he'll share the mini-bike with you. And you'll stay out of trouble.

Signed, Leeron
(your name)

....

(date)

Dear .... **,**

(character)

I know you ....

....

....

....

Before anything else happens, I want to encourage you to

....

....

....

If you do this, then ....

....

....

....

Signed, ...

(your name)

Bunnicula: A Rabbit Tale of Mystery

by Deborah and James Howe

⬧◆⬧

(ATHENEUM, 1979)

When the Monroe family brings home a strange-looking rabbit named Bunnicula, Chester the cat and Harold the dog suspect there's something dangerous about the stranger. When vegetables start being drained of color overnight, their suspicions are confirmed—Bunnicula is a vampire bunny! As the two family pets try to catch the culprit during his nocturnal meals, they run into obstacle after obstacle. Harold soon loses interest, making Chester even more determined to expose the secret and protect the family from Bunnicula. Chester's methods backfire, though, creating humorous but unfortunate consequences for the anxious cat. Told from Harold's point of view, the story introduces readers to a plot that builds and climaxes as a result of a character's imagination and related actions.

Before Reading

Ask students to imagine a classroom that includes a caged parrot. Tell them that every day students come to class, they find a fresh painting on the easel. Curiosity leads them to ask around the school to try to find out who's responsible for the artwork. But no one knows. Then they look closer and notice paint spots on the parrot and around its cage.

After describing the scenario, invite students to tell how they think the mysterious paintings got into the classroom. Most likely, some will say that the "Picasso" parrot is responsible! When students finish sharing, explain that they used their imagination to fill in the unexplained and unknown parts of the story. Then tell them that they will read a story in which one of the main characters uses his imagination to try to solve a mystery.

After Reading

Can students recall whether or not Chester ever actually saw Bunnicula draining the vegetables of their juice and color? If not, how did he conclude that the rabbit was responsible for the curious condition of the foods?

(continued)

Learning Goals

- Understand how a plot can be driven by a character's imagination.

- Explore the relationship between the initial conflict, additional problems, and resolution of a plot.

- Express understanding of the plot by creating a commercial or ad for the story.

* To help students review Chester's experiences, prepare a three-column chart with the headings "Observation," "Conclusion," and "Action." Under the first heading, have students list the things about Bunnicula that Chester actually saw; in the middle column, what Chester concluded from what he saw; and in the last column, what actions Chester took based on his conclusions.

* Discuss the information on the chart. Guide students to realize that Chester often acted on what he imagined, not on what he actually observed. Explain that the plot of this story, like that of many mysteries, is steered by a combination of facts and a character's imagination.

Giant Story Vine

In *Bunnicula*, the plot develops and grows in a way very similar to the development of a vine. In this activity, students will create a vine diagram to show how each chapter relates to the initial conflict and has a role in leading to the story's resolution.

Introducing the Activity

1. Show students a tomato and ask them how it might be connected to the story's plot. After they share, tell them that this fruit can also be connected to the plot by the way in which it grows. Describe how a tomato vine sprouts from a seed planted in soil. One leaf after another buds and grows along its stem, and then the vine produces fruit.

2. Likewise, a story plot begins with a seed and soil—a character and a specific situation. From this, the initial conflict, or stem, of the story sprouts. Soon, like leaves, new problems bud and grow from the initial conflict until a resolution (the fruit) is reached.

3. Continue to explain that, in most stories, each chapter represents a different part of the story's development. To illustrate, tell students that:

   * in chapter 1, a typically quiet household stirs with excitement over a new member of the family—a rabbit (the seed and soil).

   * The initial conflict (the stem) sprouts in chapter 2, when Chester begins to suspect that this is no ordinary bunny.

   * Chapters 3 to 8 each represent a problem (a leaf) that grows from the initial conflict.

   * Finally, in chapter 9, a resolution (the fruit) is reached and the household returns to almost normal.

4. After sharing the vine analogy, invite student groups to create giant story vines to demonstrate their understanding of plot development.

For each group:

* a tomato (or a picture of one)

* several copies of page 38

* one sheet each of light brown and red construction paper

* $2\frac{1}{2}$ - by 36-inch strip of green bulletin board paper

* scissors

* green crayons, colored pencils, or markers

Making the Story Vine

1. Give each group several copies of page 38, the two sheets of construction paper, the green paper strip, scissors, and markers.

2. Ask students to decide who will work with which part of the story vine: one student for the seed and soil, one for the stem, two or more for the leaves, and one for the fruit.

3. Have students then determine which chapters represent each part of the vine. Next, instruct them to construct their parts of the story vine following the directions below.

   ✳ **Seed and Soil:** Trim one long edge of the brown paper to resemble the ground, and then write on it the corresponding chapter heading and a brief summary about the chapter.

   ✳ **Stem:** Write the heading for that chapter on the green strip of paper, along with a brief description of the initial conflict that has sprouted.

   ✳ **Leaves:** Cut out and complete a leaf pattern for each assigned chapter, and then color the leaves light green.

   ✳ **Fruit:** Cut out a large tomato shape from the red paper and write on it the corresponding chapter heading and a brief summary of the story's resolution.

4. When finished, invite groups to assemble and display their tomato vines, as shown. Encourage students to use the vines to explain how the plot develops and grows.

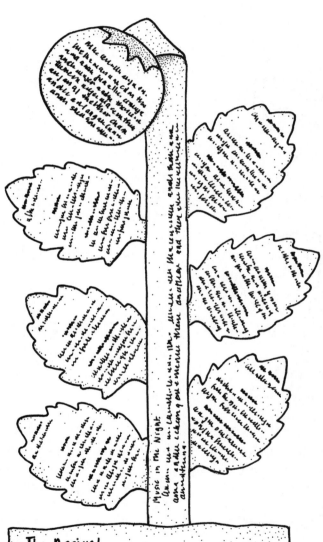

The Arrival

The Monroes bring home a rabbit they found at the movies. They named it Bunnicula after the vampire Dracula. Chester the cat gets jealous when they give Bunnicula some milk but they don't give him any.

Story
Vine Leaf

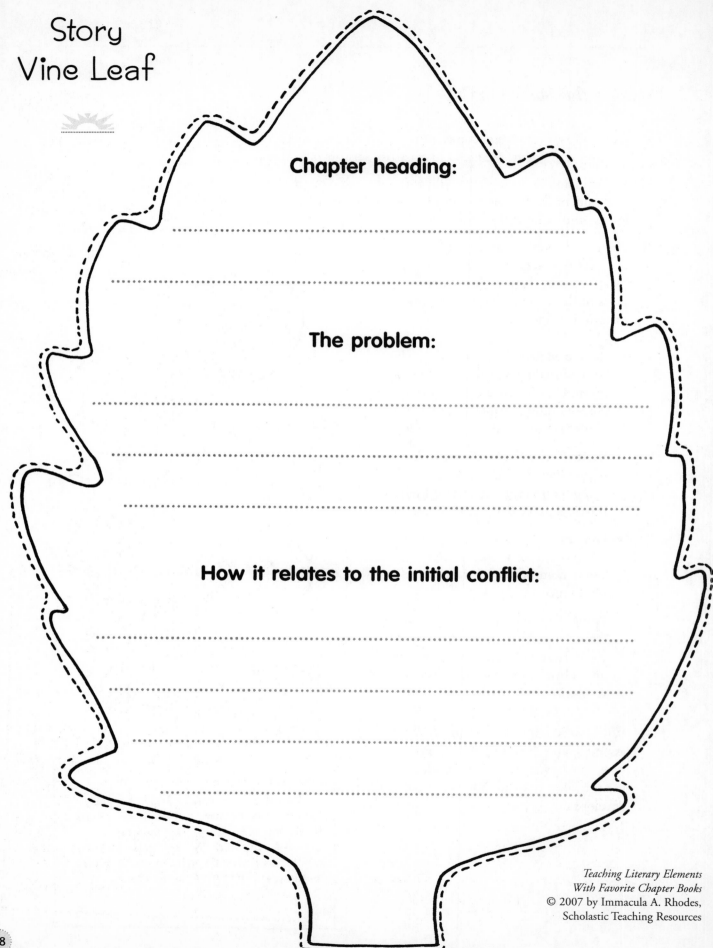

Chapter heading:

....

....

The problem:

....

....

....

How it relates to the initial conflict:

....

....

....

Teaching Literary Elements
With Favorite Chapter Books
© 2007 by Immacula A. Rhodes,
Scholastic Teaching Resources

Story Promotions

The plot of *Bunnicula* centers on the comical consequences of Chester's suspicions and fears. This activity encourages students to identify appealing and amusing events of the story and then creatively highlight these events in a poster ad or commercial to promote or "sell" the book.

For each student:

❀ writing paper

❀ 12- by 18-inch sheet of construction paper

❀ crayons, colored pencils, or markers

Introducing the Activity

1. Discuss with students how print advertisements and commercials are used to promote and sell a product. Invite them to share some of their favorite ads and what makes them so enjoyable and memorable. Are they funny? Exciting? Silly? Explain that advertisers often use humor and excitement to grab the attention of their audience.

2. Next, ask students to think about the most enjoyable and memorable parts of the plot. Are these events humorous or exciting? Can they be used in an advertisement to "sell" the story to others who have never read the book? How? After sharing, invite individuals or groups to create poster ads or commercials that will promote the story to any reader.

Creating the Poster Ad or Commercial

Poster Ad:

1. Before designing their posters, students should write the text on a separate sheet of paper. Encourage them to open with an attention-getting sentence, such as "Chester has a mystery to solve!"

2. Tell students to write a brief summary that mentions the most exciting or humorous parts of the story but does not give away the ending. Ask them to close their ad text with a creative suggestion to read the book.

3. Have students illustrate a large sheet of construction paper with colorful, interesting art that relates to the story. Instruct them to add the text, incorporating it into the art or placing it in a strategic place on the poster. Invite students to share their completed posters with classmates and then display them for other classes and visitors to enjoy.

Commercial:

1. Ask students to imagine how they might creatively promote *Bunnicula* in a commercial. Have them think about how they can highlight the main events of the story without giving away its ending. What characters will be featured and what will they do? Who will speak in the commercial? How will the commercial try to "sell" the story?

2. After mentally working out the details, students next write a script that includes the speaking parts and actions for all the characters.

3. Students can then recruit actors and make costumes and props. As they rehearse, encourage the actors to use voice inflection, facial expressions, and body language to help communicate and make the commercial's message interesting.

4. Finally, invite students to perform their commercials for the class. If desired, make a videotape of the performances to use for future literature-related activities.

Narrator: There's a stranger living in the Monroe house. No, it's not a dog that writes.

(Harold pretends to write.)

Narrator: And it's not a cat that reads.

(Chester pretends to read a book.)

Narrator: The stranger is a rabbit named Bunnicula.

(Bunnicula hops in front of Harold and Chester.)

Narrator: When Bunnicula joined the family, Harold and Chester noticed that things began to change. Could Bunnicula be responsible for the white vegetables in the kitchen?

(Harold holds up white tissue.)

Narrator: Could his unusual-looking fur and fangs mean that he's a vampire?

(Chester pretends to be a vampire.)

Narrator: Could he be a danger to his family?

(Bunnicula pretends to scare Harold and Chester.)

Narrator: There's only one way to find out— read about it!

(Narrator holds up book.)

Mr. Popper's Penguins

by Richard and Florence Atwater

(LITTLE, BROWN & COMPANY, 1938)

When Mr. Popper writes a letter expressing his interest in penguins, he enthusiastically welcomes the response—12 precocious penguins delivered to his door! But supporting a dozen penguins drains the Popper's lean finances, so the family decides to train the birds to perform. Soon the talented "Popper's Performing Penguins" take their act on the road and become an instant hit. As they travel and perform, the family and its pets have many wonderful and unusual adventures—that is, until a misunderstanding lands Mr. Popper and the birds in jail. Fortunately, a polar explorer comes to the rescue and then makes an unexpected offer to Mr. Popper and his penguins. This fun, light-hearted story features a plot driven by a series of cause-and-effect events.

Learning Goals

* Invent new solutions to problems and explore how they might affect the story plot.

* Understand a plot as a series of causes and effects.

* Express understanding of a plot by creating a story-problem game board.

Before Reading

Do any of your students have pets? If so, invite them tell about how their routines and habits may have been altered by the presence of the pet.

* Did they have to make changes or adjustments around their homes to accommodate the animal?

* Does the pet have special needs or demand more of their time, attention, or energy?

After sharing, tell students that having a pet often creates a cause-and-effect situation. For example, a dog strays from the yard so its family puts up a fence. Or a child gets a new parrot, so he has to add cleaning the birdcage to his list of chores. Ask students to brainstorm other cause-and-effect situations that might result from owning a pet.

Finally, ask them to share what kinds of problems they think might be caused by owning a pet penguin. Afterward, tell students that they are going to read about a family that has not one, but 12, pet penguins!

After Reading

1. Write the main problem of the story at the top of a sheet of bulletin board paper. Then draw a chart with two wide columns on the paper. Label the first column "At Home" and the second column "On the Road."

(continued)

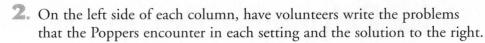
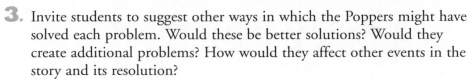

2. On the left side of each column, have volunteers write the problems that the Poppers encounter in each setting and the solution to the right.

3. Invite students to suggest other ways in which the Poppers might have solved each problem. Would these be better solutions? Would they create additional problems? How would they affect other events in the story and its resolution?

Penguin Plot Chain

Captain Cook's arrival at the Popper home became the first event in a plot filled with penguin-related cause-and-effect situations. This activity encourages students to identify and sequence the cause-and-effect events in each chapter.

Introducing the Activity

Explain that Mr. Popper wrote Admiral Drake a letter about his fascination with penguins, so the admiral sent him a penguin. From that point on, the story plot was filled with cause-and-effect situations involving Captain Cook and the other penguins. Invite students to share a few more cause-and-effect events from the story. Then tell them that they will work in small groups to create a chain of penguins on which the causes and effects of different events are recorded.

Making the Penguin Chain

1. Instruct students in each small group to assign the story chapters evenly among themselves, so that each student has several chapters to work with. Then have them cut out several copies of the penguin pair pattern on page 43.

2. Tell students to search their assigned chapters to find cause-and-effect events involving the penguins. Have them write what happens to cause the situation on the left penguin in a penguin pair, and then write what happens as a result, the effect, on the right penguin. Ask students to label the back of their penguins with the chapter number.

3. Next, each group sequences and glues or tapes its penguins together to create a chain.

4. Invite students to use the chains to retell events from the story. Later, use them to border a story-related or penguin-theme display.

For each group:

❀ several copies of page 43

❀ scissors

❀ glue stick or tape

Penguin Pair Pattern

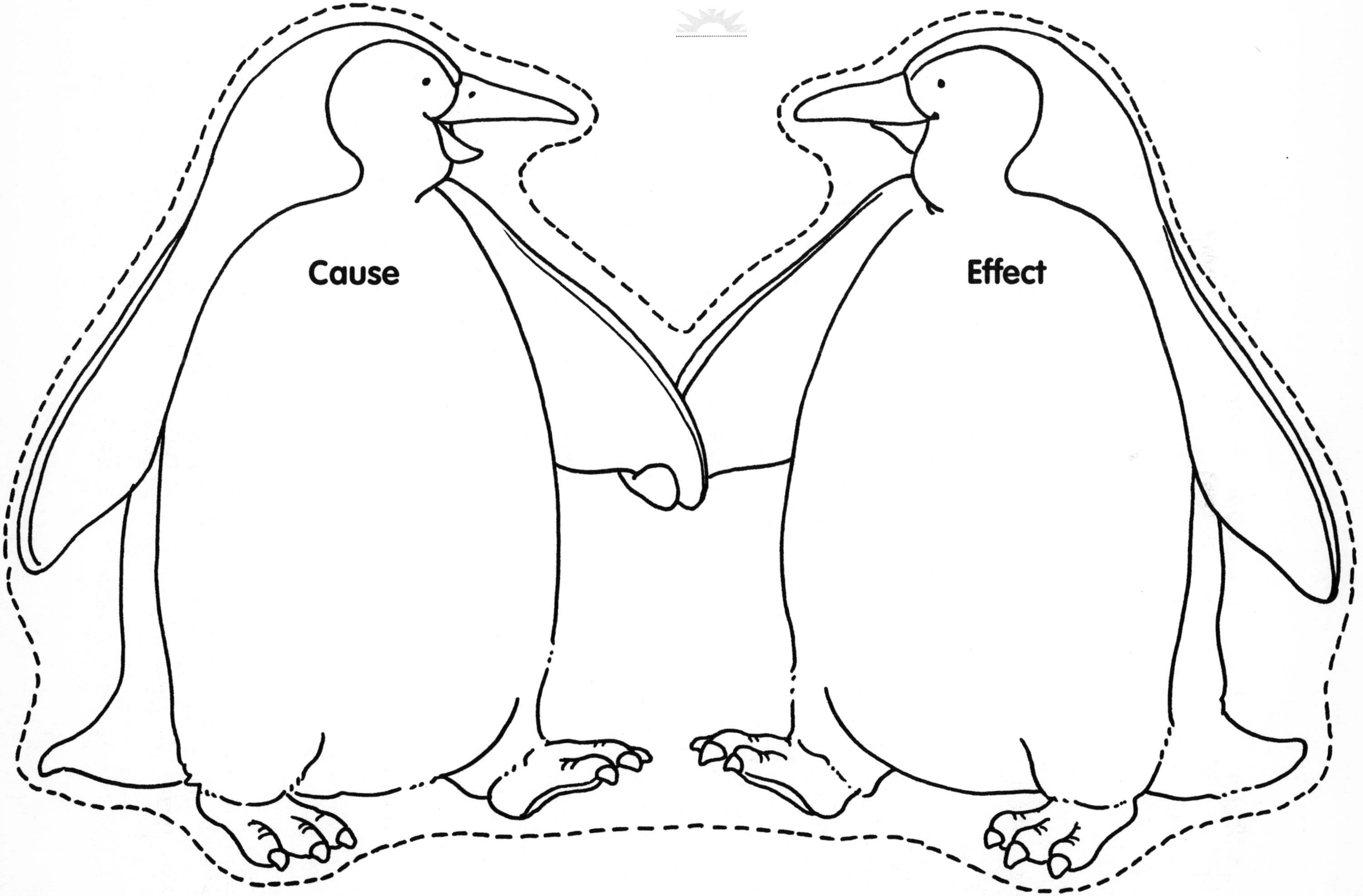

Effect

Cause

Teaching Literary Elements With Favorite Chapter Books © 2007 by Immacula A. Rhodes, Scholastic Teaching Resources

Materials

For each group:

- ✿ copy of page 46
- ✿ scissors
- ✿ 12- by- 18-inch sheet of white construction paper
- ✿ glue stick
- ✿ crayons, colored pencils, or markers
- ✿ 3 sets of five index cards, each set a different color
- ✿ large, dried lima beans
- ✿ permanent fine-tip black markers

Other Books to Use With These Activities

A Bear Called Paddington
by Michael Bond
(Houghton Mifflin Company, 1958)

The Mouse and the Motorcycle
by Beverly Cleary
(Morrow Junior Books, 1965)

Mrs. Piggle-Wiggle
by Betty MacDonald
(HarperCollins, 1975)

The Popper Penguins' Adventures Game

The plot of *Mr. Popper's Penguins* centers on the cause-and-effect situations the family encounters as a result of having pet penguins. This board game encourages students to invent other cause-and-effect events to add to different parts of the story.

Introducing the Activity

Ask students to name a few cause-and-effect events from the story. Then invite them to make up a few situations that might possibly have happened while the Popper family and penguins were at home or on the road. Ask them also to brainstorm situations that could arise during the penguins' trip to the North Pole. Afterward, tell students that they will make and play a game called The Popper Penguins' Adventures, in which the objective is to move their pieces from the Popper home to the North Pole.

Making and Playing the Game

1. Have groups of up to five students cut out the game board path on page 46 and glue it to the center of the white construction paper. Then have them draw a house, theater, ship, and the North Pole on the game board, as shown on the next page.

2. Give each group three sets of five note cards, each set a different color. Have students cut the cards in half. Ask them to assign each color to one of these parts of the story: "At Home," "On the Road," and "On the Ship."

3. Instruct students to divide the cards and write on each one something new that might happen in the story, making sure the situation fits the part of the story that is represented by the card color. Then they should label the back of each card with its category. Ask them to write at random a numeral between 1 and 3 at the bottom of each card. Next, students place each stack of cards facedown on the game board near the picture it represents.

4. Have students color the first eight spaces on the game path the same color as the "At Home" cards, the next eight spaces the color of the "On the Road" cards, and the last eight spaces the color of the "On the Ship" cards.

5. To make a game marker, let each student use a permanent marker to decorate a large lima bean to resemble a penguin and then write his or her initial on it.

6. To play, students put their game markers on the house.

* The first player picks a card from the "At Home" stack, reads the card, and then thinks of something that might happen as a result of the event stated on the card.

* After sharing the invented cause-and-effect situation, the player moves his or her marker the number of spaces indicated on the card.

* Players take turns, each time picking a card from the stack that matches the color space that their markers are on. The first player to reach the North Pole wins.

NOTE: At the end of each turn, players return their cards to the bottom of the corresponding stack.

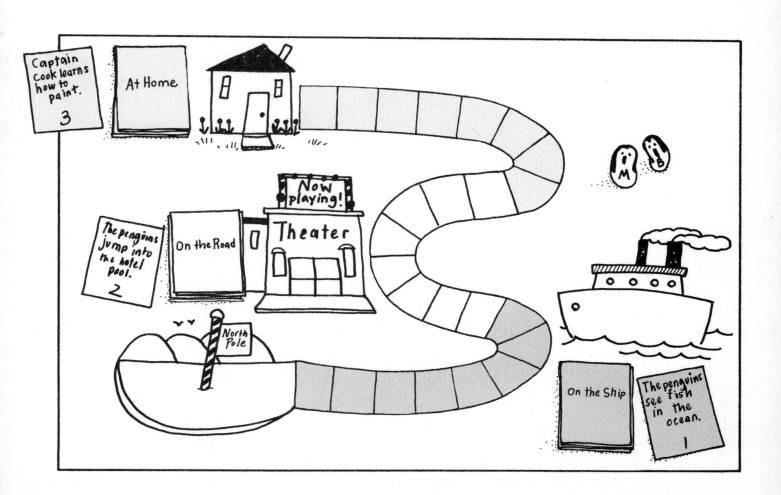

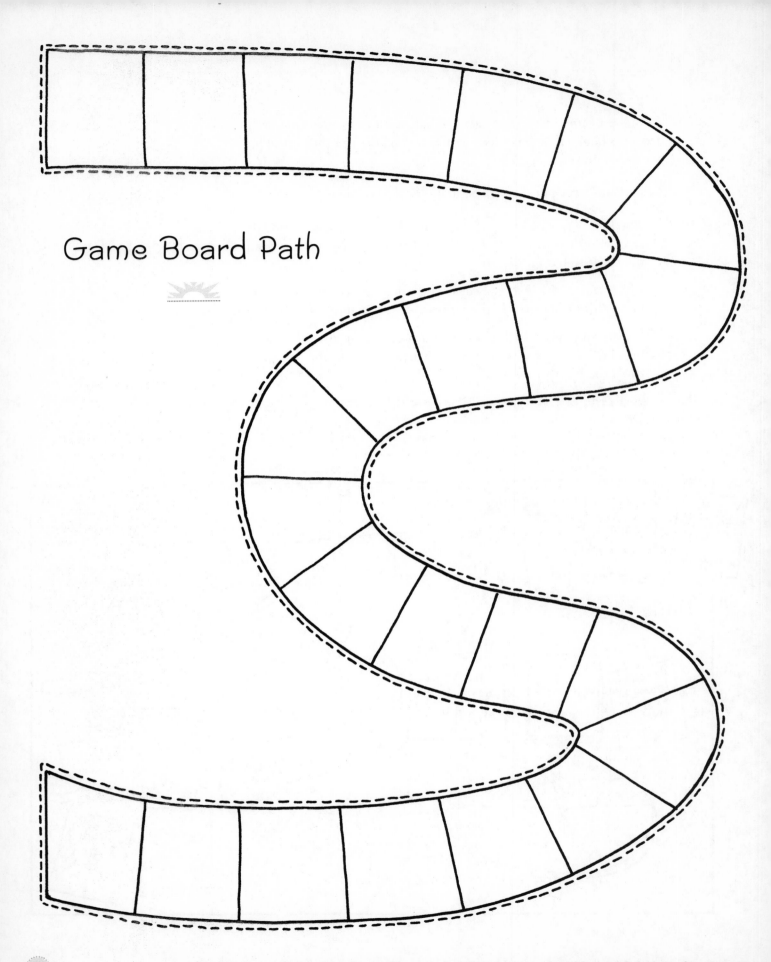

Game Board Path

Bud, Not Buddy

by Christopher Paul Curtis

❖

(DELACORTE PRESS, 1999)

After escaping an abusive foster home, Bud sets out to find his father. According to clues from a poster left by his deceased mother, the boy is confident that his dad is Herman E. Calloway, bass player for the Dusky Devastators of the Depression. In his search, the young wanderer meets with kindness, coldness, and cruelty. Finally, by relying on his ingenuity, courage, and list of personal rules, Bud locates his man—only to discover that the mean, big-bellied jazz player is not the father he had imagined! This heartwarming, humorous story introduces students to a plot in which individual circumstances and society complicate the initial problem faced by a boy who wants only to find a place to belong.

Learning Goals

✿ Understand a plot as a series of events arising from a character's circumstances.

✿ Innovate new problems by adding events to the middle of the story.

✿ Create a plot pop-up booklet based on a character's circumstances.

Before Reading

Ask students if they've ever been in situations that they'd rather not have been in, but had no choice.

✳ For example, maybe a child had to watch a younger brother or sister while the parent worked at the computer. Or perhaps a child had to go to the mall when he or she preferred to stay home.

✳ Did problems arise from these situations? For instance, did the younger sibling make a mess? Or did the child accidentally break something at the mall?

Invite students to share their experiences. Then, explain that sometimes we all find ourselves in situations that we can't avoid or change, and these circumstances often lead to other problems. Tell students that this is the case in a story about a young orphan named Bud.

Explain that the plot to *Bud, Not Buddy* is composed of a series of events that arise from Bud's circumstances. Ask students to describe the main problem of the story.

* Did Bud have any control over his circumstances at the beginning of the story? How did he try to change the situations he found himself in?

* What beliefs, rules, and attitudes during that time period created problems for Bud?

* Did he have positive experiences on his journey?

After your discussion, tell students that some story characters, like Bud, experience circumstances and problems that are caused by the rules and limitations of society; the attitudes, actions, and misunderstandings of other people; and sometimes their own misfortunes.

Expand-a-Plot Fan

In spite of his circumstances, Bud managed to overcome a number of difficulties as he searched for his father. This activity encourages students to add to the story's plot by inventing and solving new problems that Bud could have faced on his way.

Introducing the Activity

Review with students the problems that Bud faced on his journey. Then invite them to think of a few other problems that could have arisen in the story. For example, the Amoses might have taken the blue flyer out of his suitcase, the police might have caught him in Hooverville and returned him to the orphanage, or he might have met a huge snake on the road to Grand Rapids. Ask students to share ways in which Bud might solve the new problems they created for him. Then divide the class into groups of four to create these expand-a-plot fans.

Creating the Fan

1. Give the envelopes, hole punch, and paper fastener to each group. Ask students to tuck the flap inside each envelope and then punch a hole in the top left corner. Have them stack the envelopes and fasten them together with the paper fastener to create a fan. To complete the fan, one student writes a numeral between 1 and 8 on each envelope, starting with the bottom one, as shown on the next page.

For each group:

* 8 letter-size envelopes
* hole punch
* small paper fastener
* 8 white index cards
* 8 small slips of paper
* paper bag

2. Give two plain white index cards to each student in a group. Ask students to think up new story problems to write on the cards. As they work, encourage them to leaf through the book and try to create problems that can fit into a specific chapter in the book. When finished, have students insert each card facedown in an envelope.

3. Ask one student in the group to write a numeral between 1 and 8 on each of eight slips of paper. Have the student fold the slips and put them in a paper bag.

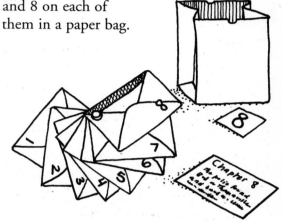

4. To use, each group spreads out the fan and places it on a flat surface. Invite a student to pick a number from the bag and them remove the card from the envelope that corresponds to that number. Ask the student to read the problem and think of a possible solution to it. After sharing, have the student set the card aside. Continue in this manner, giving each student two turns to pick a card from the fan.

5. To extend the activity, have students return the cards to the fan and then switch fans with another group.

Plot Pop-Up Booklet

In *Bud, Not Buddy*, one problem after another springs from Bud's circumstances. These pop-up booklets allow students to explore and create a short-story plot from problems that might arise from real or imaginary circumstances.

For each student:

- ❀ copy of page 51
- ❀ scissors
- ❀ $2\frac{1}{2}$-inch squares of copy paper
- ❀ crayons, colored pencils, or markers
- ❀ glue stick
- ❀ extra paper

Introducing the Activity

1. Brainstorm with students some circumstances that they might be unable to avoid or have no control over. Have them choose one of the circumstances and list several problems that might arise from it.

2. Next, tell students that the circumstance represents the main problem of a plot and the other problems are related to this main problem. Ask volunteers to tell a short story about the circumstance they chose, making sure they begin with the main problem, add a few related problems, and then end the story with a resolution for the main problem. Finally, invite students to create pop-up booklets that feature a story plot based on a character's circumstances.

- ○ the new kid in school
- ○ a new baby in the family
- ○ parents are getting a divorce
- ○ favorite teacher moves away and is replaced by a new teacher
- ○ a grandparent moves into the house
- ○ a pet runs away
- ○ parent gets a new job and moves the family across the country
- ○ best friend moves away

Making the Pop-Up Booklet

1. Ask students to cut out a separate booklet page from page 51 for the main problem, each related problem, and the resolution of their story. Tell them to cut the slits on each page.

2. Help students fold their pages, pushing the cut area toward the inside of the page to form the pop-up section, as shown. Then have them unfold each page and mark the box at the top to indicate whether the page contains a main problem, related problem, or resolution to the story. Students should write that part of the story on the lower part of the page.

3. On separate squares of paper, ask students to illustrate a separate picture to represent the part of the story on each page. Then have them cut out and glue each picture to the pop-up section on the corresponding page.

4. To make the booklet, students glue the pages together back-to-back, making sure the pop-up sections are left free. Next, have them cut out and glue a cover over the entire booklet. Ask them to title and decorate their booklet covers. Finally, invite students to share their stories with classmates.

Other Books to Use With These Activities

The Best School Year Ever
by Barbara Robinson
(HarperCollins, 1994)

Joey Pigza Loses Control
by Jack Gantos
(Farrar, Straus and Giroux, 2000)

A Series of Unfortunate Events: The Bad Beginning
by Lemony Snicket
(HarperCollins, 1999)

This is the

☐ main problem

☐ next problem

☐ solution

This is the

☐ main problem

☐ next problem

☐ solution

SETTING

The exploration of setting helps students focus on the time and place in which a story happens. Setting is the where and when of a story—it may encompass a very particular place and time, or it might involve a broad scope of faraway places and long-ago times. But setting is also much more than time and place, for it includes many other facets of a character's surroundings, such as the weather, cultural customs and beliefs, the environment, and the character's lifestyle (job, family life, economic well-being, outlook on life, and so on). Setting often has a major influence on the story's plot and what happens to characters.

An author makes a setting real by using words and phrases that appeal to readers' senses. The use of descriptive language helps students visualize the setting and imagine the sensory experiences of the characters: what they see, hear, feel, smell, and taste. The story becomes exciting and meaningful as students call upon their own sensory perceptions to interpret its mood, imagine themselves in the context of the characters' surroundings, and experience the events of the story. Exploring and interacting with setting in lively and dynamic ways enhances students' learning, increases their retention, and helps them create settings in their own writing.

The books in this section introduce students to a number of different settings. In *Sarah, Plain and Tall*, students are encouraged to explore how the author describes natural settings, and to examine life in a different time and place. *Knights of the Kitchen Table* introduces a time-travel plot, in which students focus on life in the past and how it compares to that of the present. Students are invited to interact with a fantasy setting in *Charlie and the Chocolate Factory*, while in *From the Mixed-Up Files of Mrs. Basil E. Frankweiler*, they are encouraged to examine particular places and events within a broader scope of place and time. As students explore setting with the books and activities in this section, help them focus on these learning goals:

* Use clues from the story to determine and visualize the time (past, present, or future), place, social context, or other setting in which the story occurs.

* Examine how descriptive details, sensory language, and visual imagery are used to convey time, place, social context, atmosphere, and mood.

* Explore ways in which authors make a setting meaningful, realistic, and personal to their audience.

* Discover how a story's setting can influence a character's development, actions, mood, and choices.

* Identify ways in which setting, and changes of setting, influence and help drive the story's plot.

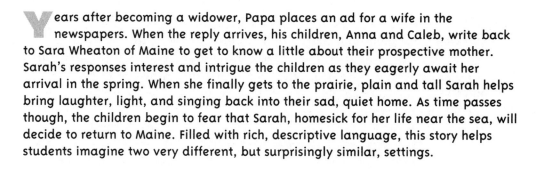

Sarah, Plain and Tall

by Patricia MacLachlan

❖

(HARPER & ROW, 1985)

Years after becoming a widower, Papa places an ad for a wife in the newspapers. When the reply arrives, his children, Anna and Caleb, write back to Sara Wheaton of Maine to get to know a little about their prospective mother. Sarah's responses interest and intrigue the children as they eagerly await her arrival in the spring. When she finally gets to the prairie, plain and tall Sarah helps bring laughter, light, and singing back into their sad, quiet home. As time passes though, the children begin to fear that Sarah, homesick for her life near the sea, will decide to return to Maine. Filled with rich, descriptive language, this story helps students imagine two very different, but surprisingly similar, settings.

Learning Goals

✿ Explore how the author uses sensory-based descriptions to tell about physical settings.

✿ Use the story's text to learn about life in an unfamiliar time and place.

✿ Visualize a setting using descriptive language from the story.

Before Reading

Invite students to share their experiences in visiting places that have features different from those around their homes. They might mention places such as the sea, plains, mountains, desert, or wetlands.

Afterward, draw a two-circle Venn diagram on the board. Label each circle with one of the settings from your discussion and the overlapping section "Both." Then have students list the differences and similarities of the two places on the diagram.

To extend the activity, ask students to diagram additional setting pairs. You might also have them draw an expanded diagram with three circles on which to compare and contrast three settings. When you have completed these activities, tell students that they are going to read about a woman who moves from the sea to the plains, and discovers that the two places are just as similar as they are different.

After Reading

Ask students to tell what they thought about the two places described in the story. Could they imagine both the prairie and the sea as they read descriptions of each? How are they alike? How are they different?

☀ Invite students to create parallel booklets to compare and contrast these two settings. Simply have them cut a stack of white paper in half and staple one stack of pages to the left side of a sheet of construction paper and the other stack to the right side.

☀ On the lefthand pages, ask them to describe and illustrate different things about life on the prairie. Then have them complete each page on the right with a corresponding description of life near the sea. Finally, invite them to share their booklets with the class.

Sensory-Setting Shadow Box

The text in *Sarah, Plain and Tall* helps the reader feel the physical setting by describing how things look, sound, and feel. In this activity, students first create a chart to list the many sensory descriptions from the story. They then use that information to create a shadow box representing life on a prairie farm.

Introducing the Activity

1. Draw a three-column chart on bulletin board paper with the headings "See," "Hear," and "Feel." Then look through the book with students to find examples of things from the prairie that the author described by how they looked, sounded, or felt. Have volunteers write each example under the corresponding heading.

2. After students have completed the chart, tell them that they will make paper shadow boxes to fill with things that represent life on the prairie during the time depicted in the story. As they work, remind students that they may use the chart as a source for ideas for illustrating the squares of their shadow boxes. To extend the activity, repeat this activity for the seaside setting.

Materials

For each student:

- enlarged copy of page 56
- crayons, colored pencils, or markers
- scissors
- glue stick or tape
- ruler

See	Hear	Feel
stars blink like fireflies	insects buzz	dandelions as soft as feathers
hair looks golden	cows rustle	sheep have thick, coarse wool
water bugs circle around	wind hisses	cool water
flowers the color of setting sun	hail sounds like stones being tossed	lambs have wet noses
cows have dinner-plate faces	cluck	sun is hot
land rolls like the sea	lightning crackles	cool hay
black and green clouds	soft rumble of thunder	
hail is white and gleaming	hammer pounding	
breath in the air	wheat whooshes	

Making the Shadow Box

1. Give students an enlarged copy of page 56. Have them draw in each shadowbox square something that represents life on the prairie. The drawings can represent things that might be seen, heard, felt, or any combination of these sensations.

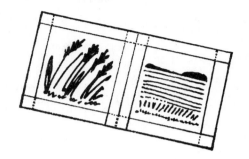

2. Have students cut out the shadow box pattern and then cut along the additional dotted lines.

3. Next, they fold the four corner tabs and sides inward along the solid lines and glue the corner tabs in place to shape the outer walls of the box.

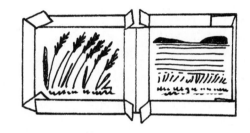

4. Direct students to fold the box back along the center solid line and then fold each side forward along the other two solid lines.

5. To complete the box, have them glue the four inside tabs to the folded sections of the center of the box, as shown.

6. To display, ask students to stand their completed shadow boxes on a table or other flat surface and share them with their classmates.

Tip

Before giving students materials for the project, it may be helpful to show them how to cut out and assemble the shadow box.

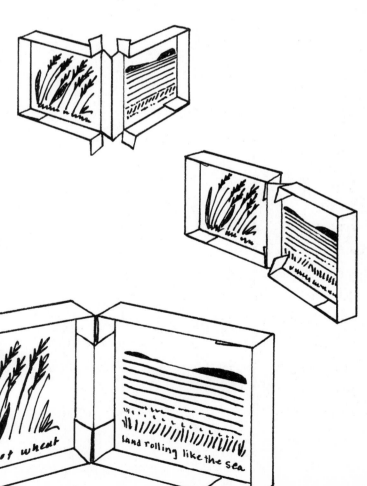

Sensory-Setting Shadow Box

Teaching Literary Elements With Favorite Chapter Books © 2007 by Immacula A. Rhodes, Scholastic Teaching Resources

Window Views

During any season, a view from the window of Sarah's prairie home most likely revealed a very different image from that of her seaside home. This activity helps students visualize a window view of each setting and then compare and contrast the two scenes.

Introducing the Activity

1. Review with students some of the prairie sights, and then sea sights, that were described in *Sarah, Plain and Tall*. If the class created a chart for each setting in the shadow box activity on page 54, use the information collected on the charts to guide the discussion.

2. Ask students to imagine a scene they might view if they looked out a window from Sarah's prairie home. Encourage them to combine pieces of information from the discussion and try to make them blend together to create a flowing, seamless mental image of a prairie scene. Then have them visualize a view from a window in Sarah's seaside home. Afterward, invite students to make window views for each setting.

Creating the Window Views

1. Ask students to pick a season and then imagine what they might see during that season if they looked out a window in Sarah's prairie home. Have them draw on a sheet of white paper the scene that they visualize. Instruct them to center and glue their pictures to a sheet of construction paper so that the colored border resembles a window frame.

2. To make window shutters, tell students to cut another sheet of construction paper in half and fan-fold each half, making one-inch-wide sections across the paper. Then have them glue a shutter to each side of the window, making sure the free edges of the shutters meet when they are pulled across the picture.

3. To create a shutter latch, tell students to close the shutters over the window and then use the sticky part of a sticky note to hold the shutters in place.

4. Repeat steps 1–3 to make a window view of a seaside scene. When complete, invite students to take turns opening the shutters on each of their windows and sharing about the view with the class.

Materials

For each student:

✿ 2 sheets of white copy paper

✿ crayons, colored pencils, or markers

✿ 4 sheets of construction paper

✿ glue stick

✿ scissors

✿ sticky notes

Other Books to Use With These Activities

The Cricket in Times Square
by George Selden
(Farrar, Straus and Giroux, 1960)

The Little House Books
by Laura Ingalls Wilder

Misty of Chincoteague
by Marguerite Henry
(Macmillan, 1947)

Knights of the Kitchen Table

by Jon Scieszka

◆◆

(V I K I N G , 1 9 9 1)

Learning Goals

❀ Explore elements that make up a fantasy world.

❀ Compare and contrast the book's world with students' own world.

❀ Create a time travel machine to compare things from one time period in the story to another.

A mysterious book transports Joe and two friends back to the time of King Arthur. When the time-travel mist clears, the boys find themselves facing a battle-hungry Black Knight. After outwitting and defeating the knight, they travel with Sir Lancelot and the Knights of the Round Table to the Great Hall of Camelot. There, posing as enchanters, they request King Arthur's help in returning home. But Merlin the Magician wants the boys to rid the kingdom of two menacing villains to prove their powers. Can they boys survive a meeting with a giant and a dragon? Will they ever get back home? Elements from the past and present are cleverly blended to create a fantasy setting for this fast-paced time-travel adventure.

Before Reading

If students could travel to the past, what period of time would they visit? Pilgrim or Revolutionary War times? Ancient Egypt? The Stone Age? The Jurassic period of dinosaurs? Encourage them to tell why they would visit their chosen time period. Then ask students to share about how life in those times would be similar to or different from life today. What things would they enjoy? Dislike?

Invite students to draw a picture of themselves during their chosen time and to share their drawings. Then tell them that they are going to read a story about three boys who travel back to the Middle Ages.

After Reading

Ask students what they thought of the story.

❋ Do they think the boys really traveled back in time? Or did they just imagine their adventures?

❋ Which parts of the story belong to the present world and which belong to the past?

❋ Which parts would probably never happen, in the present or past?

Explain that these imagined, magical, and unlikely parts make up the fantasy elements in the story. Point out that fantasy worlds often combine elements from the real world—whether present or past—and elements from the author's imagination. For example, in *Knights of the Kitchen Table*, the boys remained their present-day selves even in the fantasy world of the past.

Invite students to imagine themselves traveling back to King Arthur's time. Have them write a short story about their adventures to share with the class.

Time-Travel-Machine Settings

When the fog settled, it didn't take Joe and his friends long to notice that they were in a different time and place. This activity encourages students to compare and contrast different aspects of the two time periods from the story.

Introducing the Activity

1. Ask students to list things from the story that gave clues that the boys had traveled to another time and place. For instance, the armored knight on a horse was a sure sign that the boys had left their 20th-century world. Other clues include the clothing, transportation, buildings, and speech and customs of the people in the story.

2. Use the list as a springboard to compare and contrast things from King Arthur's time to things in the present. In your discussion, ask students to share as many comparisons as possible. Record their responses on a chart, such as the one below. Then invite them to make time travel machines to show how things can differ between two different time periods.

For each student:

- copy of page 61
- scissors
- crayons, colored pencils, or markers
- 2 paper fasteners
- glue stick or tape

In the Present	In King Arthur's Time
People wear T-shirts, jeans, and sneakers.	They wore armored suits and pointed metal boots.
People ride bicycles, cars, and buses.	They rode horses.
People live in houses in the city.	They lived in castles or huts in a kingdom.
People play baseball and watch TV.	They watched knights fight giants and dragons.
Airplanes can be seen in the sky.	Dragons could be seen in the sky.

Making the Time Travel Machine

1. Invite students to cut out the time travel machine patterns on page 61 and color the machine cutout and the knobs. Then ask them to cut the slits in the machine. Have students use a paper fastener to attach each knob to the machine.

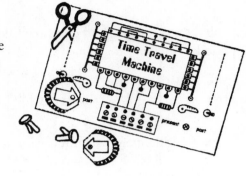

2. Have students tape the two strips together as indicated. To illustrate the strip, they should draw and label something that represents the past in each section on the left side of the strip. Have them draw a corresponding thing from the present in each section labeled with the matching number on the right.

Tip

▲▲▲▲▲▲

● In step 2, students can opt to depict present things on the left side and past things on the right side.

● Invite students to make additional pull-through strips to compare different aspects of the past and present, such as clothing, customs, transportation, jobs, and homes.

3. To set up the machine, have students thread their illustrated strip through the machine slits, as shown. Instruct them to tape or glue a tab to both ends of the strip to keep it from falling out.

4. Tell students to adjust the strip so that all the pictures on the left half are visible to the left of the slit and only the tab on the right shows out of the slit on the right. (The pictures on the right side will be hidden behind the machine.)

5. Ask students to set the left knob to indicate the time period in which the contents will be sent through the machine: past or present. Have them set the right knob to show the opposite time period.

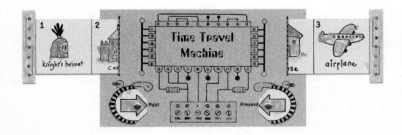

6. Students "start" the machine by slowly pulling the strip out of the right side. Ask them to tell about the picture in each section as it disappears into the left side of the machine. Then have them tell about the changes brought about by time travel when the corresponding picture appears on the right side. Finally, invite students to share their pull-through strips with a partner.

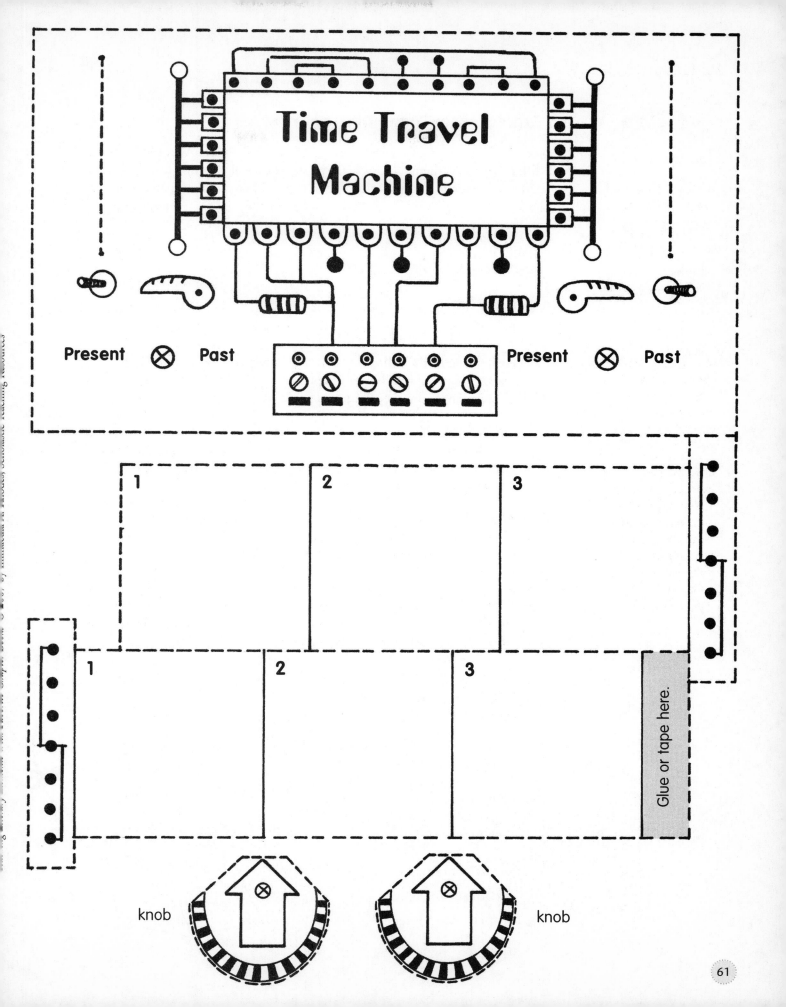

Time Travel Machine

Present ⊗ **Past**   **Present** ⊗ **Past**

1   2   3

1   2   3

Glue or tape here.

knob   knob

Materials

For each student:

- several sheets of white copy paper
- crayons, colored pencils, or markers
- stapler
- $4\frac{1}{2}$ - by 12-inch strip of construction paper
- glue stick

Talk-of-the-Times Dictionary

Joe, Fred, and Sam discovered that people in the Middle Ages talked quite differently from them. In this activity, students will examine how language helps characterize a time period. Then they will create dictionaries that include words, phrases, and expressions from the Middle Ages and their modern-day meanings.

Introducing the Activity

1. Divide the class into three groups. Give each group a length of bulletin board paper and a copy of *Knights of the Kitchen Table*.

2. Assign one of the following sets of chapters to each group: chapters 1 and 3, chapters 4 and 5, or chapters 6 and 9. Ask each group to appoint one student to be the group recorder.

3. Explain that the chapters assigned to the groups feature expressions that were used during the Middle Ages. Point out that language used during a specific time can characterize that period just as much as clothing, transportation, customs, and other elements of the time do.

4. Ask each group to review its chapters to find examples of expressions used during King Arthur's time. Have the recorders write the examples on the bulletin board paper and then circle each one with a speech bubble.

5. When the groups finish, discuss the examples and what they mean in today's language. Afterward, display all the speech bubbles for students to use as a reference when they make these dictionaries.

Creating the Dictionary

1. Tell students to cut several sheets of white copy paper in half lengthwise. Then have them fold each sheet into thirds and reopen. Direct them to label each panel as shown below.

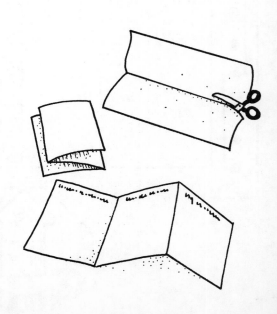

LEFT: "Word or Phrase Used Then"

MIDDLE: "Today's Meaning"

RIGHT: "My Sentence"

2. On the left-hand panel of each page, have them write a Middle Ages expression from the book (or the display); on the middle panel, what it means today; and on the right-hand panel, a sentence that uses the phrase and an illustration. Students should pick a different Middle Ages expression for each page.

3. After they finish, instruct them to stack and staple the pages together along the left-hand side and fold each page, as shown.

4. For a cover, students can simply fold the strip of construction paper in half widthwise. Tell them to title the cover "Talk of the Times" and decorate it as desired. To complete the booklet, have them glue the left panel of the last page to the inside front cover.

5. Have students open their dictionaries and read the Middle Ages expression on the left, and then read today's meaning on the right. Finally, have them unfold the right panel of the page to reveal their sentence and illustration. Tell students to refold the picture panel before turning to the next page.

Other Books to Use With These Activities

Jackie & Me: A Baseball Card Adventure
by Dan Gutman
(Avon Books Inc., 1999)

The Time Warp Trio series
by Jon Scieszka
(Viking)

The Wizard of Oz
by L. Frank Baum
(Henry Holt and Company, 1982)

Charlie and the Chocolate Factory

by Roald Dahl

❖❖

(ALFRED A. KNOPF, 1964)

Learning Goals

❀ Explore how the author uses mood to create a contrast between different settings.

❀ Create a brochure to describe the appealing facets of a particular setting.

❀ Imagine a personal experience in the book's fantasy world.

In a stroke of unlikely luck, poor starving Charlie becomes owner of the last Golden Ticket for admission to the top-secret Willy Wonka's Chocolate Factory. When the special day arrives, Charlie and the four other winners meet Mr. Wonka to embark on the tour of a lifetime. As the energetic factory owner guides them through his magical, marvelous world of chocolate, the visitors are treated to one surprise after another. But, when one child after another acts on impulse, greed, or selfishness, that child gets an unpleasant surprise. Before long, little Charlie is the only child left and that's when Willy Wonka reveals his most wonderful surprise of all! Detailed descriptions incorporate mood and the senses to make this fantasy adventure a delicious delight.

Before Reading

Ask students to name their favorite candy. Do they know how the candy is made? Do they think it might be made in some magical way and place? Encourage them to visualize an imaginary candy factory in which their favorite candy is made.

☀ Where is the factory? How would they get there? Does the factory use special machinery or workers, such as elves or fairies? Do the workers put in any unique ingredients or use a special technique to make the yummy treat?

Invite students to share some of the details of their imaginary candy factories as you write their responses on a chart. Review the ideas, guiding students to identify the things that could happen in a real candy factory and things that are make-believe. Explain that when a story happens in a place that crosses reality with elements of make-believe, it is called a fantasy.

Finally, show students the cover of *Charlie and the Chocolate Factory* and tell them that they will be introduced to Charlie Bucket, who wins a visit to a marvelous, magical chocolate factory.

1. Have students draw a picture of Charlie's home on one sheet of paper and a scene from the chocolate factory on another (they can include characters belonging to each place—such as the grandparents, Mr. Wonka, and the Oompa-Loompas). Encourage them to try to capture the mood of each place in their drawings.

2. When finished, ask students to describe their illustrations of Charlie's home. What mood did the author try to convey in the description of his home, environment, and life? Students will probably agree that the Buckets' home seemed mostly gloomy and sad. Ask them to scan the early chapters of the book to find words and phrases that suggest this mood. Some examples include "uncomfortable," "cold," "drafty," "empty tummies," "desperately hungry," and "not enough money."

3. Next, discuss some of the descriptive terms and phrases that the author uses to set the mood of the chocolate factory. Have students use similar descriptive language to tell about their factory pictures. Then have them compare the moods of the factory and Charlie's home. How do these contrasting moods add interest to the story? Conclude the discussion by telling students that mood plays an important role in the setting of some stories.

Mini-Tourist Brochure

No doubt, Willy Wonka's Chocolate Factory is a wonder to experience—and different facets of this marvelous place will most likely captivate each student! This activity encourages students to create tourist brochures that highlight the most interesting and exciting parts of the chocolate factory.

Introducing the Activity

1. Review with students some of the sights, sounds, tastes, and other sensations that the visitors experienced while at Willy Wonka's Chocolate Factory. Encourage students to share which part of the factory they would most like to visit. Why does that part intrigue them? Do they think other visitors would find it just as interesting?

2. After sharing, explain that many tourist attractions distribute brochures to highlight their most interesting and appealing points to attract visitors. The brochures often feature fun things to see and do, and also include pictures to help visitors visualize themselves in that place. Ask students to think about what they might include in a brochure to pique others' curiosity and tempt them to visit the chocolate factory. Then invite them to make mini-brochures to share with family and friends.

For each student:

- ❀ copy of page 67
- ❀ glue stick
- ❀ crayons, colored pencils, or markers

Making the Mini-Tourist Brochure

1. Instruct students to cut out the mini-brochure on page 67 and fold it in half the short way along the solid line. Ask them to glue the folded sides together, then fold the brochure along the remaining solid lines.

2. To complete the front, tell students to draw a picture of the chocolate factory in the frame and write its name on the lines. Invite them to add more text or a factory-related illustration in the space at the bottom.

3. On the left inside page, students write about a few things that can be seen at the factory. Have them illustrate some of these things in the frame shapes.

4. On the right inside page, ask students to write some other experiences a visitor might have at the factory. These can include things they might hear, touch, taste, smell, or do. Invite them to illustrate a few of these experiences in the frame shapes on this page.

5. On the back, students can list additional information about the factory, such as hours of operation, special activities, rules to follow, or advice (for example, "Wear comfortable shoes").

6. To complete the brochure, ask students to draw a map or special mode of transportation to show how a visitor might get to the factory.

....

....

....

....

....

While here, you can .....

Come and see

....

....

....

....

....

More information: ....

....

....

....

How to get there:

Visit

Materials

For each student:

❀ writing paper

❀ sheet of construction paper

❀ glue stick

❀ assorted craft materials (modeling clay, pipe cleaners, yarn, wiggle eyes, small boxes, cardboard, craft sticks, glitter, magnetic tape, and so on)

❀ crayons, colored pencils, or markers

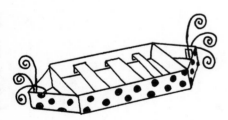

Setting Souvenirs

Often, when people visit an interesting or special place, they collect souvenirs as reminders of their experiences there. In this activity, students will write about an imaginary experience in the chocolate factory and then create a souvenir to represent that experience.

Introducing the Activity

1. Ask students if they collect souvenirs from places they visit. Why? What do they do with the souvenirs? Then ask if they ever wished to visit a place that they've read about in a story.

2. After sharing, tell students that they will make an imaginary visit to Willy Wonka's Chocolate Factory. Invite them to close their eyes and visualize themselves in the part of the factory that they would most like to visit. Encourage them to imagine all the different things they might see, hear, smell, feel, taste, and do during their visit.

3. Allow students about five minutes to play out their chocolate factory adventure in their minds. Then tell them that they will write about the most interesting part of their imaginary visit and create a souvenir as a keepsake reminder of their special experience.

Creating the Souvenirs

1. Have students write about the most exciting thing they experienced during their imaginary visit to the chocolate factory. Encourage them to describe what they saw, heard, smelled, felt, and tasted, as well as what they did. When finished, ask them to create and decorate a frame for their papers.

2. Set out a variety of craft items for creating souvenirs. Ask students to decide what kind of souvenir they can make that best represents the experience they wrote about. Ideas might include a miniature figure of Mr. Wonka or an Oompa-Loompa, a model of the glass elevator or the pink yacht, a magnet showing a scene from the Chocolate Room, or a sample of a special kind of candy or gum.

3. Invite students to share their stories and souvenirs with the class. Display them for other classes and visitors to enjoy.

From the Mixed-Up Files of Mrs. Basil E. Frankweiler

by E. L. Konigsburg

❖❖

(CORNERSTONE, 1967)

When runaways Claudia and Jamie Kincaid settle in at their new "home" at the Metropolitan Museum of Art, Claudia becomes intrigued by a small angel statue and the question of its authenticity. Knowing the answer, she was convinced, would bring about the changes she longed for in herself. But her research leads to a dead end and Jamie wants to go home, so Claudia agrees to leave. On the way, she takes a detour to the home of the statue's previous owner, where she unravels the mystery of Angel—and can finally return home "different." This story invites students to learn about life in a big city as they join the characters in the many different places of a New York City setting.

Learning Goals

- ✿ Understand that a setting can affect the story's plot.
- ✿ Explore different places that can exist within a larger setting.
- ✿ Use context clues to identify a particular place within a setting.

Before Reading

Tell students that there are times when each of us might wish to escape temporarily from the world as we know it. The desire to run away might arise from any number of reasons, such as being bored, getting angry, feeling unfairly treated, or even the notion that a great adventure awaits "out there."

Explain that there are many ways to escape—going to a special place, letting your imagination drift to faraway lands, watching a favorite movie, reading a good book, or physically running away, to name a few. Have any students ever used any of these methods, or any others, to "run away" from their worlds for a while? Use their responses as a springboard to discuss safe, acceptable, and desirable ways to make temporary escapes versus unsafe methods, such as leaving without telling an adult or running away to an unknown place.

Tell students that they will read a story about two children who run away to a special place in the hopes of becoming different in the process. (You might also add that the story occurs almost 40 years ago, a time in which safety and security concerns were quite different from those of today.)

1. Invite students to share their thoughts about the story. Do they think Claudia's plan would work in a different setting, such as in the country, in a small town, or on a beach? Why or why not? Ask students to discuss which parts of her plan might work in the different settings and which would fail. Explain that a story's setting affects everything else in the story. So if the story took place in a different setting, the characters would respond in different ways to their surroundings—and the story plot would change as a result.

2. To demonstrate, divide the class into small groups. Tell them that they will devise a runaway plan to a different setting for Claudia and Jamie, but they must try to follow the children's original plan as closely as possible. For instance, the children may not be able to travel to their destination by train, but may have to take a bus instead. Or a museum may not exist in the new place, so they might have to stay in a public library. Encourage them to think about how these differences will affect the rest of the story.

3. As the groups work, have them write an outline of their plans. After each group shares its plan with the class, invite students to discuss the pros and cons of the plan.

Snapshot Timeline

Although the two Kincaid children ran away to the big city, their adventures occurred in a variety of places found within the larger setting of New York City. In this activity, students will explore the many different places that Claudia and Jamie visited while hidden away in a big-city setting.

Introducing the Activity

1. Help students find New York City on a map. If possible, show them a street or tourist map of the city, on which the subway lines and places of interest or importance are marked.

2. Explain to students that Claudia and Jamie were able to hide themselves in the crowds of New York City. One way they accomplished this was to move about from place to place within the city. Ask students to recall some of the places that Claudia and Jamie visited during their runaway experience (they might even locate some of these on the map). Talk about how each of these individual places adds to the big-city setting of the story.

For each group:

❀ several copies of page 72

❀ bulletin board paper (about 7 feet)

❀ crayons, colored pencils, or markers

❀ glue stick

3. Afterward, divide the class into groups of eight. Invite each group to create a day-by-day photo timeline of the Kincaid children's weeklong travels within the city.

Making the Snapshot Timeline

1. Give each group a supply of the snapshot pattern on page 72 and a length of bulletin board paper. Appoint one student in each group to write "Claudia and Jamie's Week in New York City" across the top of the group's paper.

2. Ask each group member to pick a different day of the week that Claudia and Jamie ran away, from the Wednesday they left home to the Wednesday they stayed at Mrs. Frankweiler's home. Have students search the book to find the places that the Kincaid's visited on their selected day. Then ask them to draw—on separate snapshot pages—a picture of each of those places. (If students are unsure about how a place should look, encourage them to use their imagination to create their drawings.)

3. Invite students to pretend they are either Claudia or Jamie. Have them finish the sentence on the snapshot page, in their chosen character's voice, by writing the name of the place they visited and what they did there. If desired, students may write additional information about the place or their activity there.

4. Have groups glue their snapshot pages, in sequence, on the bulletin board paper. Instruct them to write the corresponding day under each picture or set of pictures.

5. To complete the timeline, students should draw arrows between each picture to create a path showing the order in which the Kincaids visited each place during their New York City adventure. Invite them to use their timelines to retell the story of Claudia and Jamie's experiences to classmates and visitors.

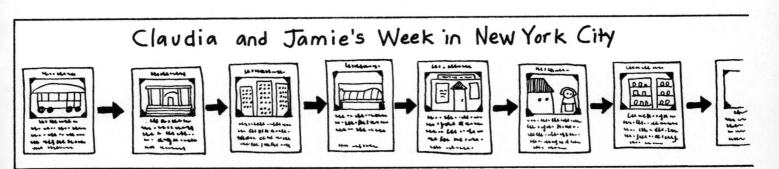

Snapshot Timeline Pattern

This is ....

(place)

where ....

....

....

....

Day: ....

Mystery Sights Cards

For each student:

🌼 2 large index cards

As they moved about, Claudia and Jamie saw some of the same things (for instance, tables and chairs) in different places in the city. One way in which an author differentiates one place from another is by describing specific sights for each place, such as stacks of books for a library, or food items for the snack bar. These things fit the context of their respective places and help readers differentiate and identify the place about which they are reading. In this activity, students will write simple visual descriptions of different places to explore how context clues help differentiate one place from another. They will then try to identify places by using clues written by their classmates.

Introducing the Activity

1. Tell students that you will describe a place in your school, and they should try to guess the identity of the place. Name a few common, visible items from your chosen mystery place: chairs, tables, walls. Can they guess the place? Most likely, students will name several different places, such as the cafeteria, classroom, art room, and library.

2. After they respond, repeat the clues, this time adding a clue more specific to that place. For instance, if the place is the art room, add easels to the description. Add food trays if it is the cafeteria.

3. After students identify the place, ask them to explain how the last clue helped them narrow down their choices to make the correct guess. Guide them to understand that many places in the school contain similar items, but they also contain things that specifically belong to that place and help students (and teachers) differentiate and identify the place.

4. After discussing some other items that help distinguish one place from another, tell students that when authors write about visual aspects of a place, they often include details to help readers visualize and differentiate that place from any other. Then invite students to make mystery sights cards to describe different places in the story for classmates to guess.

Making the Mystery Sights Cards

1. Ask students to think of a place in the story that they would like to describe (if desired, they may use the timeline activity on page 70 for ideas). Have them write on one blank card a few words or phrases that describe things that can be seen in their chosen place. Encourage them to include some things that are common to other places, but at least

(continued)

Other Books to Use With These Activities

Bridge to Terabithia
by Katherine Paterson
(Harper & Row Publishers, 1977)

The Magic Paintbrush
by Laurence Yep
(HarperCollins, 2000)

Tuck Everlasting
by Natalie Babbit
(Farrar, Strauss and Giroux, 1975)

one thing that characterizes that place specifically (for instance, tables and chairs are common to both a library and cafeteria, but stacks of books are characteristic of a library). Ask students to write four to six clues on their cards, reminding them to use clues that are accurate but will provide a challenge to others who try to guess the place.

2. Next, instruct students to write the name of the place they described on a separate card and place this card behind the clue card.

3. To use, students take turns reading their clue cards to the class. When a classmate guesses the correct place, the card holder shows the place card to verify the answer. Continue until every student has had a turn to read his or her clues and each place has been identified.

4. Group up to 10 students together and have them combine their cards. Invite them to randomly place the cards facedown on a table. Then have students play a game of Concentration, where players try to match clue cards to the proper place cards. (It is not necessary that each clue card be matched to the place card created by the same student—if more than one pair of cards representing the same place is used, they should be interchangeable.)

5. Extend this activity to help students practice writing about settings using senses other than sight. Simply challenge them to describe their chosen places by the sounds that might be heard there, thus creating mystery sounds cards. Or have them create mystery smells or mystery touch cards. In addition, students can make cards to describe and identify different places in their school or community.

THEME

Theme is the heart of a work of literature. It is the message that the story conveys about life in general. This message is not usually stated in the story—the reader must discover it by putting the story ideas and events together and examining what they learn about people, human nature, the world, and themselves through the text. And, since students bring their own backgrounds and experiences to their understanding of a story's message, each individual may focus on and identify different themes from the same story. By considering what motivates characters, the decisions they make, the consequences of their actions, and what they learn, students are able to relate the story's message to their own lives. Their interpretation of a story's theme may reinforce their existing values and beliefs, inspire them to make changes that help them grow and strengthen their own character, or even take action to improve the world around them.

The books and related activities in this section encourage students to explore a variety of themes and connect these messages to their own lives. While each book may carry an overall message about life, it is important to keep in mind that many "sub-themes" may also be communicated through the story. In *Stone Fox*, for example, the theme of determination is threaded throughout the story, yet underlying messages about self-belief and compassion also capture the minds of readers. Although friendship is the primary theme in *The Whipping Boy* and *The Prince of the Pond*, students will discover messages that address differences, prejudices, acceptance, and cooperation. And, while *Shiloh* challenges readers to develop personal interpretations about what is right and wrong, the story also encourages them to explore messages about relationships and hard work. The discussions and activities related to the books in this section help students develop the following understandings about story themes:

- Themes are the messages authors want to communicate through their stories. In fiction, themes are usually unstated and left up to readers to discover and interpret.

- Themes evolve as stories progress and are often revealed through characters' experiences, their interactions with the setting, what they learn, and how they grow or change in the story.

- Discovering themes is a personal process, and readers might interpret more than one theme from a story. Readers' understandings of themes are based on their own experiences and beliefs, views on life, behavior, feelings, and values.

- Themes often inspire readers to apply the life lessons learned by story characters to their own experiences, attitudes, behaviors, and circumstances.

Stone Fox

by John Reynolds Gardiner

❖❖

(HARPERCOLLINS, 1980)

Learning Goals

- ❀ Identify a story's message by exploring what the characters learned.

- ❀ Understand that characters experience personal rewards from what they learn.

- ❀ Share personal opinions and beliefs through letters to story characters.

Ten-year-old Willy is determined to run the farm until Grandfather is better. But in spite of Willy's hard work and loving care, the old man becomes worse. One day the boy discovers why his grandfather took to bed—tax collectors are going to take the farm away! Looking for a way to pay the taxes, Willy enters the National Dogsled Race, only to discover that Stone Fox, who has never lost a race in his life, is going to run the race, too. This short, sad tale offers students a long-lasting message about the power of love, determination, and compassion.

Before Reading

Tell students about something you had to work hard at to accomplish—for example, practicing an instrument to earn a seat in a band or training for a marathon. Explain that a person who works hard to achieve a goal has determination.

Invite students to share about times when they were determined to achieve a goal. Afterward, tell them that they will read about a boy who is determined to win a dogsled race, even though the odds are against him.

After Reading

1. Ask volunteers to tell what they think is the main theme of *Stone Fox*. Write this on chart paper. Tell students that stories such as this one often carry more than one message. What might be some messages of this story? ("You have to believe in yourself," "Sometimes grown-ups need help from children," and "It takes courage to try to do something that others think you can't do.") Write these on the chart paper, too. Discuss each response and the ways students think the author communicated that message through the story.

2. Next, divide the class into small groups. Have each group pick a message from the list. Instruct group members to work together to create a skit that demonstrates their chosen message and can be related to their own experiences. For example, to demonstrate the message that a goal can be achieved through hard work, students might develop a skit about a child who practices and practices until he can finally ride a bike without falling.

3. After they complete their skits, have students take roles and rehearse them. Finally, invite each group to perform its skit for the class.

Message Mobile

In this story, characters found their rewards in what they learned about themselves and others. These mobiles encourage students to identify some of the messages that help point characters toward a reward of personal discovery and growth.

For each student:

✿ copy of page 78

✿ 3- by 12-inch strip of tagboard

✿ yarn

✿ scissors

✿ tape

✿ crayons, colored pencils, or markers

Introducing the Activity

1. Tell students that not all rewards consist of money, prizes, or trophies. Explain that sometimes our experiences reward us in ways that help us grow and become stronger in character. We can't see or touch these kinds of rewards, but they are revealed in how we change our attitudes, values, and beliefs to become better people. Remind students that Little Willy received the prize for winning the race.

2. Then ask them what other rewards Willy might have gained through his experiences. Students might conclude that his reward was learning that it's important to believe in oneself, that one should never give up, and that a person who appears uncaring may actually be very kind. All of these discoveries rewarded Little Willy with lessons that he can apply to his life and relationships.

3. Invite students to tell about the personal rewards that other characters—such as Stone Fox, Grandfather, or Doc Smith—might have enjoyed as a result of their experiences. Then have them make these mobiles to show some ways in which characters were rewarded through what they learned from their experiences.

Making the Mobile

1. Ask students to cut out the arrow and ribbon patterns on page 78. Tell them to write on each arrow a character's name and a statement about the message that the character learned from his experiences. Then have them turn over each arrow and write about how that character was rewarded by discovering the message.

2. Have students write the book title and author name on a tagboard strip. To create a mobile, they can use yarn and clear tape (or punch holes and tie knots) to hang each arrow from the left half of the title strip.

3. Next, students color the ribbon pattern and hang it from the right half of the title strip. To complete the mobile, tell them to tape or tie a yarn hanger to the top of the strip, adjusting the hanger's position so the mobile balances.

4. Invite students to share their mobiles with the class, and then display them for others to enjoy.

Message Mobile Patterns

Character _____

Message _____

_____

Character _____

Message _____

Character _____

Message _____

Reward

Teaching Literary Elements
With Favorite Chapter Books
© 2007 by Immacula A. Rhodes,
Scholastic Teaching Resources

Multi-Message Tower

As students read a story, they most likely analyze the actions and experiences of characters and form opinions about what they should and shouldn't do. These thought processes stem from readers' own experiences, ideas, and opinions as well as the messages that are taking shape as they read. These multi-message towers invite students to share their opinions, ideas, and advice with characters and also help them discover personal lessons from the story.

Introducing the Activity

1. Remind students that several characters in *Stone Fox* played important roles in what others learned from their experiences. Write "Little Willy," "Grandfather," and "Stone Fox" on chart paper (or a whiteboard). Then have students tell how each character played a role in another character's life. As they share, ask them also to tell how each character had a part in what another character learned.

2. After looking at the relationship among these three characters, encourage students to think about what they would like to say to each one about the way he acted in the story. For example, they might want to encourage Little Willy to try hard, or praise Stone Fox for showing compassion, or express disappointment to Grandfather for giving up. Then invite them to create multi-message towers to express their thoughts to the characters.

Creating the Tower

1. Instruct students to choose a sheet of light-colored construction paper and fold their paper into thirds, as shown. Then have them write a short letter to three different characters in the story, using one panel of their folded paper for each letter. Encourage students to tell the character what they think and feel about that character's actions. Tell them their letters might also include advice on how the character should have acted.

2. Give students three blank index cards. Have them draw a picture of each character to whom they wrote on separate cards. When finished, ask them to cut a loose outline around their drawings and glue each cutout to the top of the panel on which that character's letter is written. To make the card stand up, have students use clear tape to adhere the straight edges of the paper together, creating a three-sided tower.

3. Invite students to read each letter on their tower to the class. After each letter is read, encourage them to tell what it reveals about the letter writer's values and beliefs.

Materials

For each student:

❀ 1 sheet of light-colored construction paper

❀ 3 index cards

❀ scissors

❀ tape

Other Books to Use With These Activities

Call It Courage
by Armstrong Sperry
(Aladdin Paper, 1990)

The Courage of Sarah Noble
by Alice Dalgliesh
(Charles Scribner's Sons, 1954)

Esperanza Rising
by Pam Muñoz Ryan
(Scholastic, 2000)

The Whipping Boy

by Sid Fleischman

❖❖

(GREENWILLOW BOOKS, 1986)

Learning Goals

- 🌸 Recognize how a story's message can help change our attitudes and opinions.

- 🌸 Explore a character's situation, actions, and beliefs to discover the theme of a story.

- 🌸 Express the personal meaning of a story's message to students.

Fed up with Prince Brat's intentional pranks to have him whipped, Jemmy plans to escape his post as the whipping boy. But before he can escape, the prince drags Jemmy along on a runaway adventure of his own. The boys are soon captured by outlaws who confuse Jemmy for the prince and decide to hold him—and his whipping boy—for ransom. After repeated attempts to escape their captors, the boys find themselves in the city sewers, where they finally lose the outlaws—and find a friend in each other. The unlikely bond forged between these two boys presents a strong message to students about how friendships can happen in spite of barriers such as social class and prejudice.

Before Reading

Ask students if they have ever been mistakenly blamed for doing something they didn't do, such as breaking a lamp or spilling paint on the carpet. Were they punished? How did they feel about taking the punishment for something they didn't do? What do they think the true wrongdoer should have done in that situation? Allow students to share their experiences. Then tell them that in the story they are going to read, they will meet a child prince who has a whipping boy to take the punishment for all of his pranks and wrongdoing.

After Reading

1. Use a marker to draw a large Venn diagram on a sheet of chart paper. Label each large circle "Prince Horace" or "Jemmy" and the overlapping section "Both." Ask students to name characteristics that describe each boy and his situation at the beginning of the story. Write their responses in the corresponding circles. If students name common characteristics for the boys, be sure to write these in the overlapping section of the diagram.

2. Invite students to use the information on the diagram to explain why a friendship between the prince and Jemmy seemed unlikely.

3. Ask students to identify characteristics that describe the boys and their situations at the end of the story. Use a marker of a different color to add these to the appropriate places on the diagram and to put a mark through any characteristics that no longer apply. Did either or both of the boys change? In what ways? How did these changes lead them to become friends?

4. Invite students to write a sentence summarizing what they think is the story's message about friendship, and then share their sentences with the class.

Think-About-Theme Pyramid

Authors often take their characters through some challenging experiences as they reveal the main theme of the story. This activity encourages students to explore how characters' situations, actions, and beliefs relate to the story's theme, as well as to recognize what personal message the story holds for them.

Introducing the Activity

1. Explain to students that the theme of *The Whipping Boy* is revealed through what the characters experience and how they change as a result of those experiences. In most stories, authors introduce their characters by telling about their initial situations, actions, and beliefs. The events in the story often include a twist in the characters' experiences, which in turn causes a change in their situations, actions, and beliefs.

2. Tell students that they will assemble a special pyramid that will help guide their exploration of a character's situation, actions, and beliefs in different phases of the story and will also help them discover what they learned from the story.

Making the Pyramid

1. Instruct students to cut out the pyramid patterns and chart labels on page 83. They should also cut out the opening in the large pattern.

2. To make the small pyramid, show them how to fold the small pattern along the solid lines and glue where indicated. (The text should face out.)

(continued)

For each student:

- copy of page 83
- scissors
- glue stick
- large sheet of construction paper

Tip

▲▲▲▲▲▲

If possible, enlarge the pyramid patterns and then photocopy onto heavyweight paper.

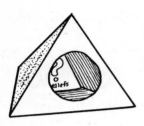

3. Ask students to fold the large pattern along the solid lines. Then have them glue one tab in place to form one point of the pyramid. Next, they drop the small pyramid into the point. To complete the pyramid assembly, have them glue the remaining two tabs in place.

4. Next, group students into pairs. Ask them to draw a three-column, three-row chart on a large sheet of construction paper and glue the labels on the chart as shown below.

5. To use, each pair picks a character from the story.

* The partners take turns shaking the pyramid to tumble the inside pyramid. After shaking, they hold the pyramid with the opening at the top (this will cause the inside pyramid to fall into the opposite point).

* Students look into the opening and rotate the pyramid so that the inside text is upright.

* Then they read the statement that faces them on the outer pyramid and complete it with the word on the inside.

* Students write their responses in the corresponding space on their chart.

* If they "roll" the same statement-word combination more than once, they either add new information to that space on the chart or roll again.

* Whenever the inside pyramid lands on "Tell what you learned," students write their response at the bottom of the chart.

6. Instruct the pairs to continue until they fill in all the spaces on their charts. Invite them to share their charts with the class.

Character: **Jemmy**

	Situation	Actions	Beliefs
Tell about the character's initial...	Jemmy was Prince Brat's whipping boy.	He secretly planned to escape and go back to the sewer.	Jemmy believed he could never, ever like the prince.
Tell what happened to change the character's...		Prince Brat made his own runaway plan and forced Jemmy to go with him.	
Tell about the change in the character's...	The outlaws thought Jemmy was the real prince.		Jemmy started to see that he and the prince were a lot alike.
Tell what you learned.	Being rich or being a prince doesn't make it okay to do the wrong things. People who are different can become close friends.		

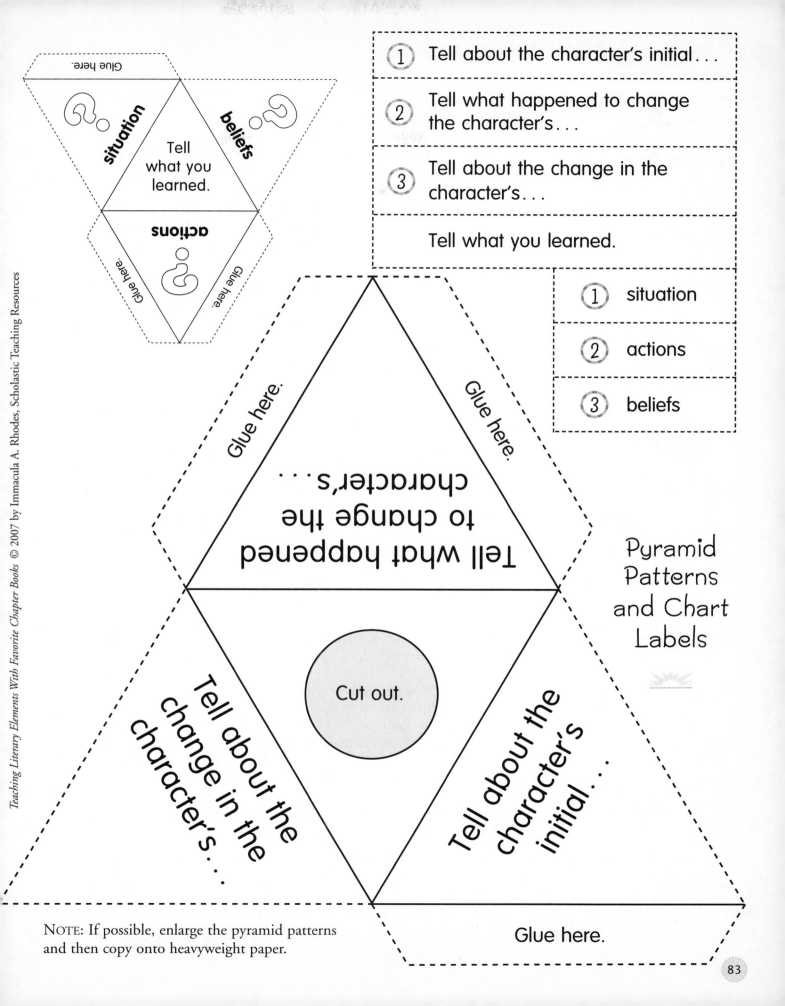

Glue here.

situation

beliefs

Tell what you learned.

actions

Glue here.

Glue here.

① Tell about the character's initial...

② Tell what happened to change the character's...

③ Tell about the change in the character's...

Tell what you learned.

① situation

② actions

③ beliefs

Glue here.

Glue here.

Tell what happened to change the character's...

Pyramid Patterns and Chart Labels

Cut out.

Tell about the change in the character's...

Tell about the character's initial...

Glue here.

NOTE: If possible, enlarge the pyramid patterns and then copy onto heavyweight paper.

Materials

For each student:

❀ copy of page 86

❀ scissors

❀ glue stick

❀ three 2-inch-wide strips of paper

Other Books to Use With These Activities

Charlotte's Web
by E. B. White
(Harper & Row, 1952)

Gooseberry Park
by Cynthia Rylant
(Harcourt Brace & Company, 1993)

Missing May
by Cynthia Rylant
(Orchard Books, 1992)

Theme Treasure Chest

Making discoveries that help us learn and grow stronger is like finding a chest of precious treasures. What characters experience and learn in literature can often guide us down the path to such discoveries. In this activity, students will create treasure chests filled with the personal messages they discovered while reading and sharing *The Whipping Boy.*

Introducing the Activity

1. Tell students that when we picture ourselves in another's situation, we often get a close-up and personal view of what that person experiences. To help them get a closer look at the characters' experiences in *The Whipping Boy*, ask them to imagine that they are Prince Horace at the beginning of the story. Have them respond to the following from the prince's perspective:

❋ Why do you misbehave?

❋ Are you proud of your behavior?

❋ Do you care about how others feel?

❋ What do they think about you?

❋ Why do you want to run away?

2. Next, tell students to imagine that they are the prince at the end of the story. Ask: "What important lessons did you learn from your experiences?"

3. Continue by having students answer similar questions from Jemmy's perspective.

4. After the imaginary role-playing, invite students to share what messages they personally discovered from the story, why these are important to them, and how they can apply the messages to their own lives. Explain that these personal messages are like treasures that students can cherish and enjoy—and that grow more valuable over time.

5. Finally, invite students to make these special treasure chests in which they can store their precious messages.

Making the Treasure Chest

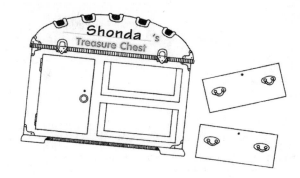

1. Instruct students to color and cut out the treasure chest patterns on page 86. Have them write their name on the treasure chest lid.

2. Ask students to glue the door and drawers onto the chest where indicated. Tell them to make sure they glue only the marked areas so that the door and drawers create pockets on the chest.

3. Give students three 2-inch-wide strips of paper. Ask them to write on each strip a personal message that they discovered from the story. Then have them fold each strip in half three times and slip it into one of the treasure chest pockets.

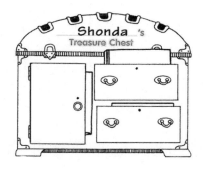

4. Invite students to share their treasure chests with a partner. Encourage them to remove and read each message and give examples of how they can apply that message to their lives. After each pair finishes sharing, have students locate another partner to share their treasure chests with.

Theme Treasure Chest Patterns

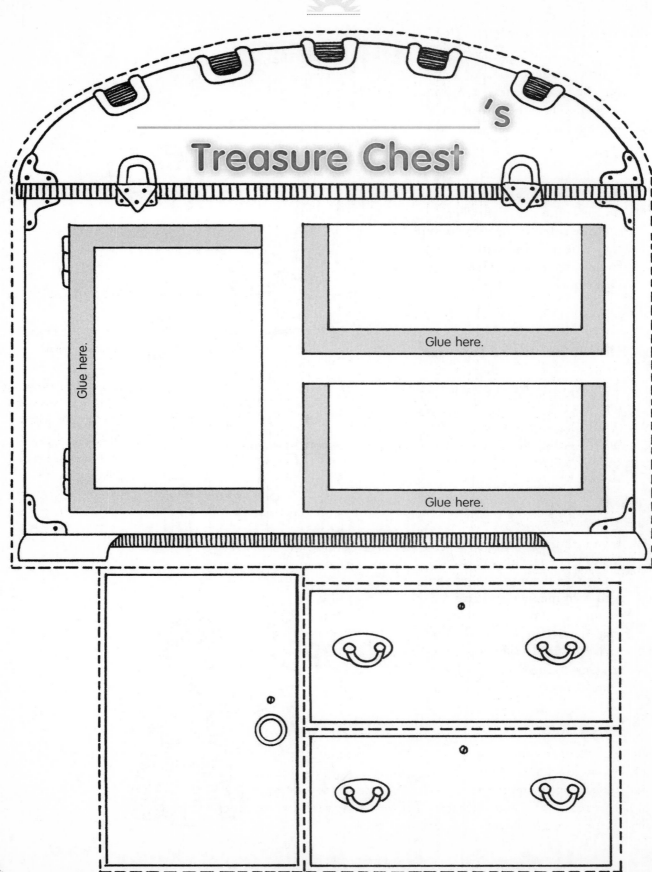

's

Treasure Chest

Glue here.

Glue here.

Glue here.

Teaching Literary Elements With Favorite Chapter Books © 2007 by Immacula A. Rhodes, Scholastic Teaching Resources

The Prince of the Pond

by Donna Jo Napoli

❖❖

(DUTTON CHILDREN'S BOOKS, 1992)

A prince-turned-frog discovers he lacks the basic instincts of a frog—he doesn't know how to hop, catch bugs, croak, or breathe underwater. Fortunately, Jade, an observant female frog, offers to teach this newcomer the life skills and lifestyles of a frog. Before long, the prince adapts to his new world and even learns to communicate—though his words are often hard to understand. But the "Fawg Pin," as the funny-talking frog calls himself, isn't the only learner in this tale. Through their experiences, Jade soon discovers that her unusual friend has a thing or two to teach her about the fascinating world of humans. This humorous twist on a familiar story offers a powerful message about accepting and appreciating others.

Before Reading

How do students think they might feel if they were suddenly changed into another creature—a frog, for example?

* Would they know how to behave like a frog?
* Would they be able to hop? Dive and swim?
* Catch bugs with their tongues?
* Communicate with other frogs?
* Survive the dangers that threaten frogs?
* How would they fit into a community of real frogs?

Guide students to understand that their lack of experience in living in a frog's world would probably create a number of disadvantages and make surviving as a frog very difficult. Show students the front cover of *The Prince of the Pond*. Tell them that this story introduces a prince who had to learn how to live life as a frog.

Learning Goals

* Relate a theme to students' own experiences.

* Use a story's message to explore personal values and beliefs.

* Recognize how a story's message can shape students' understanding of community.

Ask students what they thought of the story.

* How did they feel about Jade teaching the frog prince how to "be" a frog?

* Was she being a friend to him?

* Do they think that she accepted the frog prince's differences?

* Did the prince change his beliefs and values after he was turned into a frog? What behaviors and events indicated that the prince was still the same "person" in spite of his physical changes?

* Did Jade's beliefs and values change as a result of knowing the frog prince?

After discussing the story, invite students to share their own experiences concerning others who might have had difficulty adjusting to a new school or neighborhood or who might have looked, acted, or talked differently from them. What did they learn about themselves and the other person as a result of their experiences?

Finally, ask students to write about and illustrate their experiences and what they learned from them. After sharing their pages, help students bind them into a class book to put in the class library.

Discovery Well

Literature such as *The Prince of the Pond* helps students reach within themselves to discover how they feel, help them grow, and learn about themselves and the world. The wells in this activity encourage students to identify and "draw up" the discoveries they make about their own feelings, views, and values.

Introducing the Activity

1. Ask students why they think the frog prince and Jade returned to the well. After they share their ideas, tell them that the frogs were probably drawn back to the well because it represented a number of things to them—a place where they could feel secure and happy, where their frog family had its beginnings, where they could experience changes and solve problems, and where they could explore and express the values and beliefs that were deep within them.

2. Write "Jade" and "Fawg Pin" on a sheet of chart paper. Call on volunteers to write on the chart the values and beliefs they think the characters discovered deep within themselves.

3. After sharing, ask students to think about the feelings and beliefs that this story helped them discover deep within themselves. Then invite them to make and use these wells to express their discoveries.

Materials

For each student:

* copy of page 90
* brown paper lunch bag
* scissors
* glue stick
* hole punch
* small rock or stone (optional)
* plastic drinking straw
* 16-inch length of yarn or string
* tape
* small bathroom-size cup
* several 2-inch-wide paper strips
* small paper clips

Making the Well

Guide students in following these directions to make their wells:

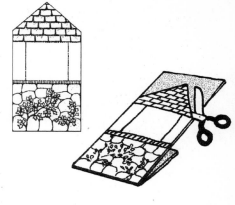

1. Color and cut out the well pattern along the outer dotted lines. (Tell students they will cut out the opening later.)

2. Glue the well pattern to the flattened bag, aligning the bottom of the pattern with the bottom of the bag. Trim off the excess portions of the bag around the roof.

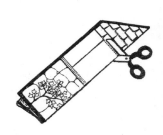

3. Lightly pinch the bag lengthwise to start cutting out the opening. Carefully cut out the opening through all layers of the bag.

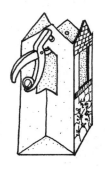

4. Open the bag and punch a hole in each side of the roof, as shown. (To make the well more stable, place a small rock or stone in the bottom of the bag.)

5. To make a well crank, knot the yarn or string around the middle of the straw, and then tape the knot to the straw to secure it. To attach a "bucket" to the crank rope, tape the loose ends of the yarn to the cup as shown.

6. Insert the ends of the straw crank into the holes on each side of the well, from the inside. Then glue the peaks of the roof together to seal the top.

7. To use the wells, give students several 2-inch-wide strips of paper. Have them write on the strips things that this story helped them discover about themselves. Then have them roll each strip, secure the end with a paper clip, and place the paper roll in their well bucket.

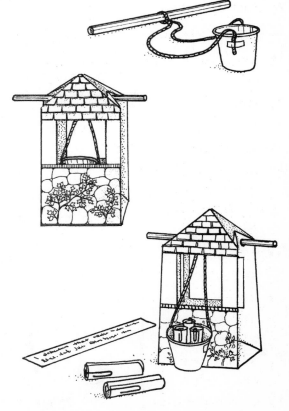

8. Students then exchange wells with a partner and take turns drawing up their partner's well bucket, picking a paper roll, and reading the statement on it. Afterward, the well owner shares a little more about the statement drawn from his or her well. When finished, students pick another partner to share their well with.

Discovery Well
Pattern

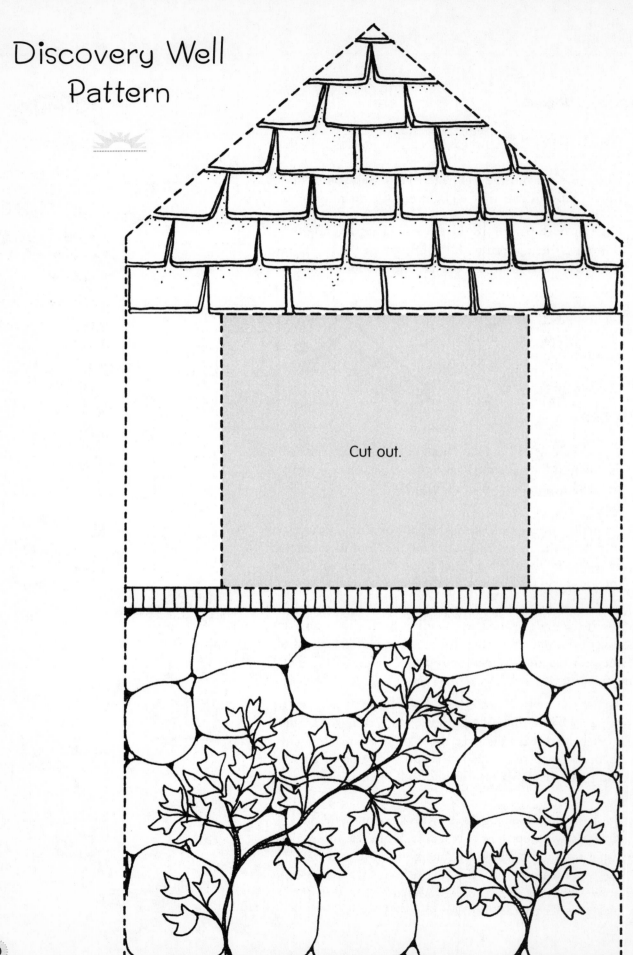

Cut out.

Teaching Literary Elements With Favorite Chapter Books © 2007 by Immacula A. Rhodes, Scholastic Teaching Resources

Peaceful Pond

Sharing the frogs' experiences in *The Prince of the Pond* can inspire students to look at others' actions and situations from a new perspective, strengthen their relationships with others, and grow their understanding of what makes a strong community. This activity invites students to express what they learned from the story about living and working together as a community.

For each group:

- blue bulletin board paper
- drawing paper
- crayons, colored pencils or markers
- scissors
- glue sticks or tape
- green construction paper

Introducing the Activity

Share with students that the frog prince and Jade learned to adapt to, accept, and appreciate each other's behaviors, abilities, values, and beliefs. In spite of their differences, they discovered that they could live together peacefully, and they even developed a special respect and love for each other.

Their attitudes and actions probably also helped strengthen the frog community at the pond. Ask students to list some examples set by the two frogs that might have made the frog community stronger. Their responses might include:

- The two accepted each other—differences and all.
- They learned from each other.
- They worked together to overcome problems.
- They cared about what happened to each other.
- They considered each other's feelings.
- They watched out for and protected each other.

Have students tell what they can learn from the story about what makes a strong and peaceful community. Encourage them to think about how they act and the things they believe that help them live cooperatively and peacefully with others at home, at school, and in the community. Invite students to work together to create a pond community in which they can express the messages this story tells about living with others.

Creating the Peaceful Pond

1. In advance, cut out one large pond shape from blue bulletin board paper. Display the pond in an area where there is ample wall space for students to decorate around it with plants and animal life. Then help them list different categories of things that they want to include in their pond scene. The list might include land plants, land animals, water animals, water plants, and insects.

2. Divide the class into the number of groups equal to the categories in the list. Have each group pick a different category and ask students to

(continued)

Other Books to Use With These Activities

The Summer of the Swans
by Betsy Byars
(Viking Press, 1970)

The Tale of Despereaux
by Kate DiCamillo
(Candlewick Press, 2003)

The Trumpet of the Swan
by E. B. White
(Scholastic, 1970)

draw and cut out pond-related items that belong to the category chosen by their group. For instance, the water animal group might create fish, frogs, turtles, and snakes. Have students add their creations to the pond display to help create a scenic pond community.

3. Show students how to cut out a lily-pad shape from a folded sheet of green construction paper, being careful not to cut the fold. Inform them that their pond community represents a peaceful pond. Ask students to write on the front of their lily pads a statement telling what they learned about living with others. Then have them open the lily pads and write on the inside examples of their personal experiences or story events that relate to their statements.

4. Invite students to share their lily pads with the class and add them to the pond scene. Post the title "Peaceful Pond" to complete the display.

Shiloh

by Phyllis Reynolds Naylor

(ATHENEUM, 1991)

When Marty first meets Shiloh, he returns the dog to his owner. But when Shiloh reappears, Marty is convinced that he's been mistreated, and he secretly vows to keep the dog and earn enough money to buy him. One night Shiloh is attacked—and Marty's secrets are exposed! Will he lose Shiloh? Will his parents ever trust him again? Can he face the owner and demand the right thing for Shiloh? As Marty struggles with these questions, he learns valuable lessons about honesty, responsibility, and respect. By sharing Marty's experiences, readers will explore their own beliefs about right and wrong and what they value.

Learning Goals

- Express personal beliefs about issues that involve making right and wrong choices.

- Explore a theme that addresses a character's struggle between right and wrong.

- Create statements to express a story's theme.

Before Reading

Have students name some school rules, such as "Walk in the halls," "Respect each other's property," and "No fighting on school grounds." Explain that rules tell us how we should behave in different situations. They are designed to provide safety and fairness for all.

Then ask students if there are times when it's okay to break a rule. If so, under what circumstances? For example, is it okay for a student to run in the halls to report an emergency to the school office? Or to fight a student to make him or her stop bullying another child?

Expand your discussion to include situations in which students might make an exception to the rules or behavioral expectations of your community. (Is it right to claim another person's property if he or she mistreats it? To lie to protect someone from being physically harmed?) Encourage students to explain their responses. Afterward, tell them that they will read a story about a boy who must choose between right and wrong in order to protect an abused dog.

After Reading

Ask students to share their reactions to the story. As they read the book, did they develop their own ideas about what Marty should do? Invite volunteers to tell which of Marty's choices they agree with and which they disagree with. For the choices with which they disagree, what would they suggest that Marty do instead? How would the new choices affect the outcome of the story? Conclude your discussion by asking students to tell what they think is the message of the story and why they think this message is important.

Materials

For each student:

❀ copy of page 95
❀ scissors
❀ glue stick

Two-Sided Opinion Fence

In *Shiloh*, Marty had two confusing and complicated choices: return Shiloh to his abusive owner or keep him in a secret hiding place. In his mind, the boy played out the consequences of both choices before making his decision about what to do. This activity encourages students to consider different sides and consequences of a character's choices and then to express and explain their own views about them.

Introducing the Activity

Tell students that Marty built a fence to pen in Shiloh and keep him hidden. This fence also symbolized the secrets that he was keeping from his parents and Judd Travers. He kept his secrets inside the fence while trying to make everything look normal and right on the outside.

Invite students to share their opinions about whether Marty made a right or wrong choice to keep Shiloh secretly (they will probably give mixed and conflicting opinions). Afterward, tell them that many issues can be viewed from different sides—often we base our opinions on the side of the "fence" from which we view the situation, as well as on our own experiences, beliefs, and values. Then invite students to make opinion fences to identify and express their own opinions about a character's choices in the story.

Making the Fence

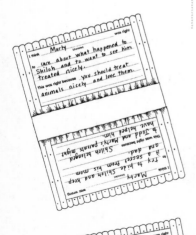

1. Ask students to think about some of the hard choices that different characters faced in the story. For example, Marty had to choose whether or not to keep Shiloh when the dog returned to him; Ma had to decide when she would tell Dad about Marty's secret; and Judd had to decide whether or not he would keep his bargain with Marty.

2. Have students cut out the fence pattern on page 95 and pick a character who, in their opinion, made at least one right choice and one wrong choice. Ask them to complete the "right" side of the fence pattern by writing about the character's right choice and explaining why they think it was the right thing to do. Then have students complete the "wrong" side of the fence by writing about that character's wrong choice.

3. Show students how to fold their fence along the middle solid lines. To create a stand-up fence, they'll glue only the top edges of each side of the fence together.

4. Invite students to share their opinion fences in small groups. Encourage them to share their views on each situation, and to explain whether they agree or not with the statements on the fence. Also ask them to offer alternative "right" choices for characters to make in place of those that they view as wrong.

I think .... was right

(character)

to ....

....

....

This was right because ....

....

....

....

....

This was wrong because ....

....

to ....

(character)

I think .... was wrong

Materials

For each student:

❀ sheet of white paper

❀ crayons, colored pencils, or markers

❀ ribbon or yarn

❀ scissors

❀ large basket (1 for the class)

Other Books to Use With These Activities

Number the Stars
by Lois Lowry
(Dell Publishing, 1989)

Pictures of Hollis Woods
by Patricia Reilly Giff
(Wendy Lamb Books, 2002)

Poppy
by Avi
(Orchard Books, 1995)

Words-of-Wisdom Scroll

Among the things that Marty discovered through his experiences was that life's problems do not always have clear-cut solutions and that nothing is as simple as you think it is. When students discover important nuggets of truth such as these, the message often sticks with and influences them throughout life. In creating these scrolls, students will shape an important message they learned from the story into words of wisdom to share with others.

Introducing the Activity

1. What important life lessons do students think Marty might share with them about his experiences? After sharing their thoughts, ask students to tell what important message they learned from the story and why it's important to them. Explain that the messages we discover from our own and others' experiences help us grow, learn, and become better people—and we can share these lessons with others to help them grow, too.

2. Invite students to shape an important message they have learned into their own words of wisdom and then use their statements in special scrolls to share with others.

Creating the Scroll

1. Ask students to think about what they learned about life from the story. Then have them work with wording the message so that it is expressed as a wise saying or proverb. For example, they might develop statements similar to these: "Hard work brings respect to the worker"; "Keeping a promise makes one proud and happy"; and "Telling lies robs a person of peaceful sleep." After students shape their statements to express the message they wish to communicate, have them write their words of wisdom across the top of a sheet of white paper.

2. Invite students to illustrate their papers with pictures and symbols that represent their words of wisdom. They might also create a border that symbolizes the message. To make scrolls, have students roll up their papers and tie a length of ribbon or yarn around them. Then ask them to deposit their scrolls in a large basket.

3. To share the scrolls, invite one student at a time to pick a scroll from the basket, unroll it, and then read the message to the class. Encourage the scroll's owner to share any additional comments about his or her scroll. After all the messages have been shared, display them on a bulletin board titled "Words of Wisdom." If desired, also add the acronym "WOW!" to the top corners of the display.